Do Black Women Hate Black Men?

Do Black Women Hate Black Men?

A. L. REYNOLDS III

HASTINGS HOUSE
Book Publishers
141 Halstead Avenue, Mamaroneck, NY 10543

Library of Congress Catalog Card Number 93-080522

ISBN 0-8038-9360-4

Printed in the United States of America

2   4   6   8   10   9   7   5   3   1

This book is dedicated to my father, Dr. A. L. Reynolds, Jr., who led me through my rites of passage and taught me to be an independent free black man, yet be tolerant of those who lacked such a benefactor.

Acknowledgments

Numerous people have helped me through the course of identifying and collecting the information that was necessary to finish this manuscript. Illinois State Senator Richard Newhouse, Judge Marion Garnett, Judge Judy Mitchell-Davis, and Leo M. Zinn were very helpful with their suggestions about how to confront those persons who are in a constant state of denial that covers up the problems. In addition, through their suggestions, I found many doors opened that helped me put together the focus groups and interviews.

Although I attempted to maintain an unbiased and objective eye on the problems described in the manuscript, at times I felt an intense negative impact beginning to weaken my resolve. It was in these many moments that John Moore of Moraine Valley College, Ted Davis of Olive Harvey College, and G. Scott McCarthy of Chicago State College would fortify my determination to continue and complete the exploration of the problems. Our frequent conversations and informal get-togethers energized me throughout the interview and focus group process.

Jeanette Branch, a psychiatric social worker and vice president of TWO (The Woodlawn Organization), was extremely helpful, and the inclusion of focus groups was her idea.

With regard to the technical aspects of the manuscript, there are three people whom I feel indebted to. First Elaine LaWell, who at times functioned as both my right and left hands, transcribed the many pages of interviews and notes, and typed the manuscript. No amount of thanks would be sufficient for her tireless efforts. Ralph Rieves's help on the manuscript was invaluable. Once I was able to get him, a white friend since childhood, to recognize that the problems facing black men do exist, he critiqued every chapter and endured countless discussions concerning the existing crisis and conflicts of which I was writing. But more valuable was his contribution in giving me a white professional perspective. His patience was exceeded only by his friendship throughout the entire process.

I owe a special debt to my editor and publisher of Hastings House, Hy Steirman, whose perception, insight, and knowledge of writing and publishing have taught me much. I would like to thank him for his exemplary commitment and professionalism for "getting it right."

Contents

Author's Notes

Until the 1950s, strong relationships existed between black women and black men. They were the major factor in keeping racism from destroying the black family and the black community in America. Now, it has been replaced, in many instances, by a war between the genders—a war in which there can be no winners. The real casualties will be the black families and black children of America.

The title, *Do Black Women Hate Black Men?*, though provocative, is not meant to incite anger or frustration. The intent of the book is to promote self-awareness, spur positive community action, and change attitudes in black America. Of course, not all black women hate black men or vice versa—but too many black women have been hurt, abused, abandoned, left pregnant, helpless, and homeless by black men who refuse to accept responsibility for their marriages or their relationships; hence, the reason for this anger by black women.

As a psychologist, I have to search for deeper meanings.

A book by a political philosopher headed me in the right direction by pinpointing the reason for the rift: Professor Andrew Hacker, in his best-selling book, *Two Nations, Black and White, Separate, Hostile, Unequal*, states:

> The real change began during the Second World War, when for the first time black Americans were courted by white society. A shortage of civilian labor forced employers to offer jobs to workers who had previously been excluded. More than a million black women left domestic service never to return. At the outset of the war, blacks [men] were drafted into the armed forces to serve in labor battalions. By its end, they were given the right to fight and die and many did.

I had often been "told" that black Americans had fought in every one of our country's wars, including the American Revolution. But I had to find out for myself, so I tracked down the statistics:

Washington's Continental Army =	5,000
Civil War, Union Army =	200,000*
World War I =	367,000
World War II =	1,000,000
Vietnam War =	274,937
Persian Gulf War =	104,000

Yes, black Americans have fought and died in every war since the American Revolution. After World War II, the

---

* 38,000 were slain in battle; 22 won the Medal of Honor

GI Bill of Rights gave veterans a chance to go back to school. It also freed black men from low-paying jobs and allowed them access to colleges or technical training. It should have been the first step toward better jobs and better pay. It wasn't. Though some black men did succeed, many more didn't. This accelerated the civil rights movement.

Meanwhile, progress for black women outpaced that for black men; as black men were in uniform, black women were rising in the workplace. More opportunities opened up for them. Then, many black women embraced the Women's Liberation movement, which further separated them from black men as they sought, at long last, equality in the home as well as in the workplace.

Thus, black men felt not only the sting of discrimination and lack of opportunity in a white society's job market, they also were being looked down on by the now better-educated, better-paid black women, as well as the vocal black Women's Libbers.

Except for the emotionally strong black men, this had a disheartening effect on the black men anchored to lowly job opportunities, those who lacked the training to compete for jobs with black women. The final blow came with the war in Vietnam. Again, thousands of eligible young black men went off to fight. Those who weren't killed, wounded, or traumatized came back to the same limited opportunities in a biased society. The future was bleak. The lack of jobs equated with poverty. For these disenfranchised black men, the only "job" opportunities for earning a living and achieving self-esteem were drugs and crime.

The newly educated black females found there were now fewer eligible, educated black males to meet their rising expectations as they sought potential mates. While women were growing in social status, the men could not keep pace. There were fewer role models for young boys, as the sexes kept moving in opposite directions. The communities suffered as black marriage rates dropped; today, 58 percent of all black families are headed by a female. Often, young black men with fewer strong black role models in the family turn to crime for status, money, and attention.

Maya Angelou said it best in a recent TV interview with Charlie Rose:

"There is a schism which exists between black men and women, and it's really painful and frightening because we were taken together from the African continent. We lay spoon fashion, back to belly, in the filthy hatches of slave ships, and in our own and each other's excrement and urine. We stood up on the auction block together. We were sent to work before sunrise, came back after sunset together. We have been equals and we are in danger if we lose that balance because if women begin to feel, 'The black woman is the strongest—,' then where is the man? If the man begins to feel, 'I have no place in her life,' then there's no balance, and all our people will have paid all those dues for nothing."

The result is that today, black men are becoming an endangered species, while strong black families are decreasing in numbers every year. What can be done to stop the disappearance of responsible black men? How do we stop the war between black men and black women? What constructive measures can be taken to cure this cancer that is daily eating away the foundation of the black family? Black men must survive, and must restore black family unity. But how?

As outside forces continue to erode personal relationships, psychologists have pointed out that some black men restore their own manhood by mistreating women. In retaliation, black women confess that experience has taught them to get what they can out of relationships— because sooner or later, their men will either depart, leave them pregnant, or abuse them. One young woman writing in the *Wall Street Journal* told of her five sisters, all of whom had been beaten or abused by their husbands and lovers and then abandoned. Even rappers have taken to ridiculing black women, calling them bitches and "hos" (whores) who should be beaten and raped.

These are some of the problems I will address in this book. The situations described in the following case histories were selected from over three hundred interviews I conducted in black communities across America. The situations cited are intended to show the nature and extent of the antagonistic relationship between black men and black women. My interviews were nondirective and open-ended with cluster samples representative of all groups of black America. The narratives and case histories are not pleasant and will elicit revulsion and denial among some readers. My only intent is to provoke self-awareness and issue a call for action and change in black America.

It is a rare black American who doesn't know many blacks with the behavioral characteristics described in the chapters about Sapphire and Achilles. There are few black Americans who would care to admit that they, themselves, share these traits.

There are some blacks who would be more comfortable blaming this battle of the sexes solely on the black underclass. While it's true that the black underclass is saturated with these battles, it is equally true that the war exists among blacks in the labor class, and in the knowledge class. Since the knowledge class makes up less than one-fifth of the total black population in America, there is little doubt that the issues addressed in this book pertain to the majority of African-Americans.

This book is written for all black Americans, whether they wear blue collars, pink collars, white collars, or no collars.

I would like to acknowledge four books that were published during my research and the drafting of this project. Each of these exceptional works was an inspiration. Sharrad Ali's *The Black Man's Guide to Understanding the Black Woman* spurred me to sharpen my discourse about the threat of extinction. Nicholas Lehman's *The Promised Land* reinforced my belief that self-knowledge and discipline are the only hopes to solving a moral and mortal crisis. Lehman's observations about post-Reconstruction effects on the black family structure were enlightening and focusing. Nathan Hare's *Crisis in Black Sexual Politics* reflects the black knowledge class's inability to admit and deal with the crisis of black male/female relationships. Alex Kotlowitz's work, *There Are No Children Here*, is a poignant story and leaves no doubt about the nation's health.

It is my hope that there will be more books by others to throw light on the problems confronting black America that, in time, will shed more light so, again, "we shall overcome."

Every American should address the issues openly. The destructive behavior described in *Do Black Women Hate*

Black Men? should neither be tolerated nor encouraged.
No institution, organization, or political leader can
change our communities for the better until African-
Americans take absolute responsibility for their own behavior.

A. L. Reynolds III

Methodology

Although the specific cases presented can be viewed as anecdotal, much of the data and information collected and presented were extracted from over three hundred individual interviews, plus hundreds of focus groups held in both small towns and large cities, including Peoria and East St. Louis, Illinois, Gary, Indiana, Milwaukee, Wisconsin, St. Louis, Missouri, Detroit, Michigan, Nashville and Memphis, Tennessee, Chicago, Illinois, Washington, D.C., New York City, and Los Angeles.

The open-ended individual interviews produced frank and candid information on personal life experiences. Because everyone was assured that his or her identity would remain anonymous, the interviews were very candid and forthright. The focus groups, which were arranged through community, political, religious, business, professional, and personal contacts, and which varied in size from as few as four participants to as many as twelve, were also assured anonymity. These countless hours of discussion produced a no-holds-barred open exchange about the current crisis between black men and black women today. Although each group seemed to take on a life of its own, there was consistent agreement, often unspoken, that they, black women and black men, by definition, must become the catalyst and the implementer of their own solutions.

Foreword

While no one will know for certain exactly what happened between Anita Hill and Clarence Thomas, their confrontation on TV before the Senate Judiciary Committee was a startling spectacle. Here was a black female law professor accusing a black male judge of sexual harassment.

The black community, though proud of these two distinguished black combatants, was bewildered by the sideshow antics of white U.S. senators on either side of the debate, with U.S. president George Bush siding with Judge Thomas. When the Senate voted fifty-fifty on the confirmation of Thomas to be associate justice of the Supreme Court, Vice President Quayle, with the deciding vote, clinched the confirmation for Thomas.

It was heady stuff, indeed, for Americans to see two blacks involved in the highest reaches of power in America. And while Judge Thomas may have won the political battle, Anita Hill won the emotional battle—that of a woman (not just a black woman) who stood tall, fighting for her rights.

What should have been a shining example to African-Americans that black men and women with education and hard work could reach the heights in America was simply a false impression. The truth is that today, black women outpace black men educationally; for every one hundred black women who complete their college education, only sixty-seven black men get college degrees.

Though higher education leads to better jobs and better pay, it also leads to a form of elitism. Educated black women prefer educated black men, so with a growing "knowledge" class of women and a shrinking source of supply of eligible black males, an antagonism has arisen.

For men, this fracturing of their self-esteem is fueled by a need to prove themselves worthy—along with an ego need to put down these "uppity" women. This leads to confrontation, anger, and despair.

It began long before World War II when black families, especially in the South, sought to protect their daughters from becoming domestic servants and concurrently, the unwilling mistresses of the heads of white households. Families made the difficult decision to send their daughters off to boarding schools and colleges while their brothers worked at day labor to finance their sisters' education. Thus began the "knowledge" class of black women and a schism in black families that is now being expressed in antagonistic behaviors.

After World War II, some black ex-servicemen went back to school, but more, seeking better jobs, headed North to become part of America's new industrial workforce—until their world came crashing down as industrial jobs evaporated and the Rust Belt grew. What emerged next as job opportunities for young black males were either service jobs at minimum wages on one side versus a lucrative life of crime and drugs. Black teenagers with little or no education and no future were suddenly earning up to $50,000 a year tax-free.

The disastrous results were inevitable. Today, 500,000 black males inhabit U.S. prisons, further depleting the availability of young marriageable males. Young boys are growing up in fatherless homes with no guidance or direction. While Mother is at work, the young boy learns to steal and is rewarded by the one who is the most important figure in his early life, his mother (not necessarily the birth mother, but the one who stands in her stead). Is there any wonder that stealing becomes the natural part of his behavior? If a child is rewarded for lying and made part of the conspiracy, he soon learns that honesty is not always the best policy.

How did this come to be? If we accept that a child's social behavior is learned, then we start at the beginning, no matter where that may be. And we know for too many of the African-American males, this social behavior is learned in a setting that is ultimately destructive.

If a black family is to be "whole" again, the young black male must have a father to be a role model, teach him right from wrong, and to administer discipline. It is imperative that young blacks attend school, go on to higher learning, and compete in the job market.

A. L. Reynolds believes there can be no government sponsorship to cure the scourge now threatening the very existence of the African-American community. The healing has to take place from within and must be based on the willingness to acknowledge, first, the responsibility all black males and females owe to each other and to our children; second, there has to be a willingness to sacrifice in order to survive. This sacrifice means lending vision to the children, demonstrating in our daily lives those kinds of social behavior that contributes to the strength of our community.

Fifty years ago, 62 percent of all young black women were likely to get married; the birth control pill changed social and sexual attitudes, and today many black women reject marriage. Currently, only 22 percent of black women marry, while 70 percent of young black women, despite the Pill, are having children out of wedlock.

The author, psychologist A. L. Reynolds, has led hundreds of focus groups around the country to identify what is wrong with black America. He has come up with some startling answers.

DANNA WOOD,
Columbia University School of Social Work

Do Black Women Hate Black Men?

CHAPTER

1

Introduction

The plight of the vanishing black American male, which is contributing to the diminishing number of healthy black American families, is a major domestic problem in America. It is not a problem that can be solved by the federal government, or even by a majority of the population working toward a solution.

The main obstacle is that the problem has its own problem, that of a segment of our people who fail to recognize that there's a problem in the first place.

The best analogy comes out of a book on logic. If your house is on fire, you would call the fire department. But before you call the fire department, you have to recognize there is a fire—that is, you take the initiative to save your life.

The situation with black America today is comparable

3

to the person in a burning building who calls the fire department, then fails to get out of the house.

Another parallel situation would be to compare black America with a person being attacked in a dark alley. The victim has four choices:

1. He can accept his attacker's blows and be a victim. The chances are he will lose his life.
2. He can scream for help and hope he'll be rescued.
3. He can take the high moral ground and try to persuade the attacker to stop, i.e., "to do the right thing."
4. He can refuse to be a victim and take charge of the situation "by any means necessary," as Malcolm X once said.

I feel strongly that the last choice is the only choice for black America.

After twenty-five years of clinical counseling, conducting focus groups around the country, being involved in community action groups as well as small business development, I have watched the disintegration of the black family. It makes me sad, frustrated, angry, dejected, and ready to climb walls.

At the present rate of acceleration, one can project the disappearance of the black community from America in the foreseeable future. Like the weather, everybody talks about it, but nobody does anything about it. I am dedicating my life to trying to stop it. As the saying goes, "It is better to light one candle than curse the darkness."

Through black groups, fraternal organizations, church groups, and a series of good friends, I have attended focus groups across the country. I have listened, questioned, and probed ordinary folks and listened to their complaints.

I have come to the conclusion that the major threat to extinction is the antagonism between black men and black women. The common interests upon which to build a lasting, loving, and trusting relationship are slowly disappearing.

This book is entitled *Do Black Women Hate Black Men?* The opposite is also true: "Do black men hate black women?" These two attitudes preclude the survival of black America.

The first part of the book examines the destructive dynamics. The latter chapters suggest solutions.

The Black Man's Death Row

"We have seen the enemy, and he is us," said Walt Kelly's Pogo.

Although racism is destructive to black people in America, it falls far short of the destruction caused by the conflict between today's black woman and black man. This battle is producing a large number of casualties, while destroying the foundations of our race. Their conflict is black America's major enemy.

Relationships between black men and black women are marked by anger and distrust. Their conflict is black America's major enemy. An old African proverb goes, "If there is no enemy within, the enemy outside can do us no harm." The major harm to black Americans doesn't come from racism, though that is a part of it. It doesn't come from lack of jobs, political control, or lack of affirmative action, although that, too, is part of it; nor from the presence or absence of government programs. It comes from the enemy within, the present-day relationship between the genders.

The reasons for this conflict must be accurately addressed, analyzed, and solved in a practical way. Not to do so will cause the genocide of the black American male and the end of the African-American community.

If black youths are to grow into men who can establish strong families, then the present relations between most black women and black men must change.

There were 936 people murdered in Chicago in 1992, of which 70 percent were black American males. According to the National Center for Health Statistics, for the six leading causes of death among the total adult population in the United States, the black man leads the list in each category. This includes heart attacks, cancer, strokes, accidents, homicides, and suicides.

The black man doesn't need to be sent to prison to be on death row. He's there already.

In addition to the other leading causes of death mentioned, add:

Low self-esteem is killing him.

Sex is killing him.

Stress is killing him.

Low Self-Esteem

The black male is not conceived and born with attributes that make him less educable or less employable than any other person, male or female, black, white, yellow, or orange. It is only after he is born that he is shaped either into a solid citizen or into becoming less of everything considered positive in America and more of everything negative.

Many black men have low self-esteem because they grew up in a female-dominated environment. The inability (for many reasons) of their fathers to form strong families has created this situation: over 58 percent of all black households are headed by black females. In all of these families, there is no strong black role model. Even in many of the remaining 34 percent of black households, the dominant role of the male is questionable.

According to *Black Americans, A Statistical Source Book* (1990 edition), in 1975, there were 1.5 million more black women employed in the labor force than men; by 1985, that number increased to over 2 million. This same source points out that since 1980, there are more black women with high school diplomas, college degrees, and advanced degrees than black men. This number keeps increasing every year as the black man falls farther and farther behind.

The head of the household, usually the mother, explains that the family is willing to help the black female attend high school and college instead of the black male because the family does not want the daughter to end up working as a domestic. The rationale that emerges from my focus groups is that the black male can fend for himself by the time he is an adult and the black female cannot.

The black male is left alone to take his chances. The irony of this rationale is that there is no family member (particularly a male) around who is able to teach him how to take his chances.

In most circumstances, he learns (usually on the streets) that he has no chance of succeeding.

No chance leads to low self-esteem.

Low self-esteem leads to self-destructive activities.

Sex

The notion that blacks are more sensual and possess a higher sex drive than other races has been proven false. *What is true* is that sexual relations between black men and black women are more perilous than sexual relations between men and women of other races. The danger exists because most black men and black women approach a relationship with incompatible agendas.

The Achilles Syndrome

Sex is the one thing most black men believe they control. From slavery through Reconstruction, the black man was conditioned to believe that the only domain that belonged to him alone was sex. So, the black American male began to feel that he had no power over anything but sex. Deep down, because of low self-esteem, he feels insecure about his woman. But one thing he does own is his sex organ. Its use, for temporary dominance of the female sex partner, overrides his whole value system. It's a condition that is common among members of all classes. Education and experience outside the underclass are supposed to bring some judgment about behavior; nevertheless, this liability is the black man's Achilles' heel. Achilles was the warrior in Greek mythology who was invulnerable to harm, except for his heels. He died in battle when he was wounded in the heel. The moral of the story is that no man is invulnerable, because we all carry around a fatal flaw.

Thus, the black man became obsessed with sex and women. The main importance of cars, clothes, and money is to attract women for sex. Former D.C. mayor Marion Barry admitted this to *Jet* magazine in the June 3, 1991, issue. "It wasn't the drugs or the liquor. It was the sex." He admitted that was the real addiction that caused his downfall.

During a guest appearance on the Sally Jessy Raphaël show, Barry told the audience, "You get caught up in it. . . . The ego gets into it and the grandiosity, the conquests. The women. This disease is cunning, baffling, powerful. It destroys your judgment."

Marion Barry addressed the one weakness that is common among most black men, an obsession with sexual dominance. As a result, these men share a marked inability to resist sexual enticement.

What are the consequences of promiscuity and unsafe sex? Read your local newspapers.

The Sapphire Syndrome

Most black women don't measure their womanhood by sex, but by how much better off they are materially than their girlfriends. Their wants and desires are based on what they "think" the white woman has, wears, or looks like. The black woman is much more into the white world than the black man. She spends a great deal of her time shopping at malls and looking at soap operas. Her self-esteem is measured on the basis of how close she can match her perception of what the white woman has. Any black man available to be used for this purpose is her potential target. In an attempt to get what she wants, the black woman has learned to use whatever is at her disposal. Her body and sex are her ultimate weapons.

These black women seem compelled to scheme about ways to get gifts and money from men. Women who exhibit this behavior are generally classified as "Sapphires," after the nagging wife of George Stephens in the radio and TV series *Amos 'n' Andy*. In the black community, this evolved into "Sapphier," which is commonly accepted as a term meaning "conniving bitch."

Stress

Obviously, the black man's definition of manhood and the black woman's definition of womanhood create an impossible situation. If these attitudes start young, and continue as men and women get older, then honest relationships are impossible, breakups are inevitable.

When the breakup occurs, Sapphire has lost control of the man she was accustomed to using, manipulating, and deceiving to achieve her selfish goals. What's left for her? First, she still has herself, which she loves more than anything. Secondly, she has only to replace him with another black man who can give her what she wants. She doesn't necessarily have to love the man, or perhaps even respect him. She loves what she thinks he can give her, what she hopes she can get out of him, and what controls she has over him. Any feelings she possesses are all on the surface and, like a tumbleweed, they blow away with the first wind of displeasure, usually over material things.

Does the young woman learn it from her peers?

From her mother?

Their attitudes toward young black men on the make result in the approach "Give me what I want, and I'll give you what you want."

Achilles will react more severely to the terminated relationship. When he loses her, it is a public statement that he's not able to satisfy her. He has lost control over "his" woman and therefore he is nothing. The man finds little relief in knowing he lost the only thing he thought he had, his manhood.

If the attachment is not based on character and emotion, the woman has little reason to dwell on her loss. She will look for another man who will give her more clothes, more presents, more gifts. If she can't find one, she may be obliged to return to her former companion or settle for a lesser one. In this kind of situation, it's "If you can't get what you want, take what you can get."

If she feels any pain from the broken relationship, she doesn't think it matters. Even if she loved the guy, she'll make up for it. She thinks that if she can get her material gifts from the next man, why would she miss the one she left?

"Donna" describes this process very clearly in the Case of I Want Out.

"He wasn't doing that much for me, though we had been seeing each other for three years," she began. "I told him I wanted to stop seeing him so I could get on with my life with somebody else. We were riding in the car on the Dan Ryan Expressway and he started sobbing and sniffling like he was crying. First of all, I can't stand a weak man and so I just told him I was sorry but it was over," Donna stated.

"That fool said I made him feel so bad that he felt like driving the car into one of those big semitrucks coming down the highway and I just told him fine, but let me out first. When he finally got me home, I was shaking," she admitted.

"He could kill himself, but he wasn't going to kill me. I mean, sure I was sad, but you give me a couple of days to shop in the malls and go out with some of my male associates and I will be fine," she bragged.

True, maybe the relationship was at an impasse and should have been terminated. But after an intimate relationship of three years, here was Donna, a woman who has built a shell around her feelings. She lacks sensitivity to his feelings because she reveals she is self-centered and is filled with self-aggrandizement. Even seeing him overcome with grief produced no sympathy on her part. As a matter of fact, she took it as a sign of weakness. An older, successful black businessman has described this attitude: "Sapphire will pour a bucket of scalding water on a drowning man if you let her."

Of course, one cannot assume from Donna's story that all black men are sensitive and loving, while all black women are hard-hearted Hannahs. But if the norm in the black community is for young men to "love 'em and leave 'em," it seems reasonable for the girl to retaliate by trying to get something more substantial out of a relationship. This leads to mutual animosity, which escalates as each

one builds new relationships on the reefs of the previous one.

It is also true that some men are simply trying to "make
out" and don't care if they break some girl's heart or leave
her pregnant or just leave her. In any case, the schism
keeps widening, yet there has been no attempt by black
leaders to confront and then try to heal the anger fester-
ing between young black women and black men.

A True Axiom

Why won't black America confront this issue of incompatible agendas? It was Sigmund Freud who said, "Understanding the problem is halfway to solving it."

Until black men and black women confront the problem instead of each other, this deadly circle of toxic relations will remain unbroken. Neither gender is more at
fault than the other. There is equal fault and equal blame.
This is not a question of "Which came first, the chicken or
the egg?" It is a matter of the chickens coming home to
roost!

CHAPTER

3

᪣᪥

Pick a Class

Class distinctions in America generally are based on inherited wealth, the magnitude of current income, or the
wielding of economic power or political power. Is the
unhappy relationship between black men and women
present in the highest income levels of the upper class?

For all intents and purposes, there are very few black
Americans in the highest income levels of the upper class.
Less than 2 percent of black Americans are even in the
lower levels of the upper-income class. This would include established business men and women, mega-
millionaires in the TV, movie, and music industries, and
baseball, basketball, and football stars. But there are other
people with high class status, like black military leaders,
political and/or government leaders, educators, scientists,
and diplomats.

Class distinctions among blacks can be misleading if we

use wealth as the criterion. An uneducated and unscrupulous drug lord may have a very affluent lifestyle, but won't share the same community and cultural interests as an educated person. A better method of black classification would be by education. Using education and training as criteria, we can characterize black America by three classes: the *knowledge class*, the *labor class*, and the *underclass*.

The Knowledge Class

This class is made up of individuals with marketable talents, training, skills, and college-level education. The members of the knowledge class tend to be conspicuous consumers in the areas of housing, automobiles, personal grooming, and the pursuit of cultural activities. This upper level may include entrepreneurs or people who work in the arts and publishing, or as teachers and social workers.

The Labor Class

This group, while not affluent, maintains a steady income by working full-time at those jobs that may or may not require some college education, but does require perseverance. This can range from sales to policemen/firemen, car production and steel mills. Frequently, members of the black labor class work at lower-paying jobs that no one else will do. They may own some property and assets. They may share some of the interests of the knowledge class, yet live in areas populated by the underclass.

The Underclass

The black underclass is made up of individuals whose social and economic experiences have convinced them that there is only a marginal place for them in mainstream America—that of the perennial victim. They manifest feelings of powerlessness and hopelessness. Members of the black underclass generally live in neighborhoods where rates of crime, poverty, low educational achievement, crowding, disruption of family life, and probability of substance abuse are highest. Health statistics demonstrate that they experience higher than average rates of physical illness and have a shorter life expectancy. Other major sources of stress for the group include prolonged unemployment, disruption of marriage through separation or divorce, high numbers of single female parents, and a high incidence of premature or abnormal births.

Common Values and Treachery

The knowledge class and the labor class share common values as well as interests. There are married and unmarried couples of both classes who have mature and enduring relationships characterized by love and trust. But there are far too many members of both classes who are caught up in the Sapphire and Achilles syndromes.

The examples that follow show that discontent between the sexes permeates all three classes of black Americans.

Lorraine, an administrative assistant to the director of

the Board of Health of a midsize city in the Midwest, is a twenty-nine-year-old, light-skinned, very attractive black woman. Although she dates white men, she prefers black men.

Lorraine became romantically involved with Leo, a thirty-five-year-old bank officer who bore a striking resemblance to the actor Billy Dee Williams. After about ten months of involvement, Leo noticed that Lorraine had started pointing out to him jewelry and clothes that she thought would look good on her. Though enthralled with the relationship, Leo didn't get the hints.

Early in their courtship, Lorraine had given Leo a very nice pair of shoes from Neiman-Marcus and a diamond ring worth, she let him know, an estimated $1,800. During this same period, Leo had taken her to Nassau for a week, bought her a poodle for $600, and paid $1,600 for white wall-to-wall carpeting that Lorraine wanted for her apartment.

Leo was accustomed to taking Lorraine to rather elegant restaurants on the weekends, as well as to plays and concerts. He usually would spend between $100 and $150 each weekend on their entertainment.

Although he had experienced many black women asking him for money and gifts, he was not interested in grasping women. So he became very impressed with Lorraine's apparent independence and her values. He felt they had a lot in common and found himself very much in love with her to the point he was about to ask her to marry him.

"She never used to ask for anything until after the tenth month," he said. "I was not ready for what happened in April. She asked me to lend her ten thousand dollars for a down payment on a BMW. She had an excellent position, and I knew she had money in the bank, so I asked her why she didn't get a car loan from the bank. Lorraine told me that if I lent her the money, she could pay me back in trade. Can you imagine how I felt? I told her I'd think about it.

"To add insult to injury, she added that if I wouldn't come up with the money and take payments in trade, she knew someone else who would.

"Hey, I was messed up for a long time after that," he said. "After all those words of love and how much she cared, I was shocked at the type of woman I'd almost married."

It is interesting that Lorraine felt she had to build up credits with Leo. First the shoes and then the ring were given to him to encourage him and then she moved in for the $10,000 kill. It is also interesting that Leo was caught completely unaware. He was so infatuated with her, he missed the fact that Lorraine was taking his gifts and nights on the town for granted. As a member of the knowledge class, Lorraine exercised her manipulation in a subtle manner.

There are many black women who are not as skillful as Lorraine, yet have raised their standard of living within the labor class. A perfect example of this is the Case of Slick.

Slick is the nickname her mother gave her when she was four years old, and although her friends know her as Mahogany, her given name, her nickname is much more fitting.

Slick is attractive and lives with her mother and father, a sister, and Slick's twenty-four-year-old daughter.

Although she has never worked and never lived outside her parents' home, Slick has never been on welfare. At age forty-two, she has bedroom furniture, a TV and VCR, and her own telephone. Slick is accustomed to demanding that her man of the moment help her. She demands that they pay her money each month if they want her to be nice to them.

She claims she got pregnant in the backseat of a car when she was eighteen, then dropped out of high school just before graduation. The baby's father, a steelworker in Milwaukee, would bring gifts and money each month for Slick and the baby, while her married boyfriend would provide money for her social needs.

Slick has had a total of four married men who have taken care of her since she was fourteen years old, and she has slept with any man who would spend money on her.

Lorraine and Slick aren't that different, even though one is from the knowledge class and one is from the labor class. Too many black women practice and perfect manipulative lifestyles that range from Lorraine's to Slick's. They spend most of their waking hours perfecting techniques to use on the black man. They are sharpshooting Sapphires who can hit an Achilles' heel from fifty yards.

The tragic saga of Anthony Riggs illustrates what destruction this behavior can bring when it is taken to the extreme in the underclass:

Anthony Riggs, a twenty-two-year-old black man returning from an eight-month tour of duty in the Persian Gulf War, survived the war only to end up a murder victim. According to *USA Today*, Anthony Riggs had written a letter to his mother complaining about his wife. "I don't know what is on her mind. . . . Mom, I would put my head through the neck of a hot sauce bottle to please her."

When Riggs returned from the Gulf, he discovered that his wife had emptied his bank account of $8,000 and wrecked his car. In addition, she greeted him with a request for a divorce and $500 in monthly alimony. She was four months pregnant. Emotionally distraught, Riggs asked his wife to account for her behavior. A few days later, he was killed by five gunshots.

His wife and her brother have been indicted for his murder.

The Reverend Jesse Jackson is quoted in *USA Today* as calling Riggs's death "another product of this culture of violence." Such a vague commentary on this incident defies logic and precludes any concrete solution. Even worse, it lets the real agent of death off the hook.

It was *not* a culture of violence that harmed Anthony Riggs, but the toxic relationship between a black man and black woman. His wife was from the underclass of black women who haven't developed the ability to cope with their own behavior.

The situations described in this chapter are actual and representative. They are the unfortunate norm in many black communities and classes. As a result, there are millions of black Americans who are disadvantaged regardless of their class.

4

Meet Achilles

Sexuality is probably the least understood aspect of human behavior. Its common feature is the procreation drive that is shared by all animals. Sex as related to self-identity is an aspect peculiar only to humans. It is this aspect that makes the study of human sexuality so complicated; nevertheless, there are accepted norms of human behavior. Promiscuity is a deviation from accepted norms, and in many instances, promiscuous behavior can be attributed to neurosis.

Achilles' behavior, as discussed in chapter 2, is characterized by an obsession with sexual conquest. It is a myth that the black race possesses some inherent biochemical trait that increases the sex drive. It is a fact that many black men have a neurotic sex drive. Why? Because promiscuity among these black men results from an inner need that is almost a compulsion to prove their "manhood." There are extremes of this behavior that can only be described as irrational.

Bread and Bed

The prisons and jails are populated with *black males who are there not because they were trying to feed their families, but because they needed to feed their loins*. The black man in prison didn't get the money he was going to use to buy those clothes, that car, or the gifts. Instead, he got the time "because he committed the crime." If you want to hear a cry for help from a hapless man who knew better, here is how Derrick describes it in the Case of Bread and Bed.

"You gotta have bread if you are going to get her to bed, man. Ain't no doubt about it," Derrick says. "Shit, I was twenty-three when I went in and twenty-eight before I came out of the joint. I just plain stuck up some people. Look, the bitches aren't going to deal with you if you can't pay. I mean, they look at your clothes, your ride, your shoes, and all that. If you ain't got no ride, they ain't going nowhere with you.

"I could eat on what I could hustle but I couldn't feed *them*. I'd have a hard-on in the morning, afternoon, and night, and the sisters wouldn't give me no play until I had some bread," Derrick admits.

"There is a lot of home boys in prison just like me. They doing good time, just like I did. They can get out with half their time. I got ten years but only served five. The bitches I was dealing with didn't even visit me, but that's yesterday's news 'cause a lot of dudes are in prison with no visitors. I'm probably going to be back in the joint. Right now, everything is cool. I hustle a little dope and that keeps some kind of money in my pocket, and the women are crazy about this 'caine. So I can get over right now, unless I get busted," Derrick says.

Derrick portrays the picture of a lonely black man waiting for a disaster. He admits that he is going to do whatever he has to do to get a black woman, even if it means he expects to go back to prison. He will even employ narcotics to have sex with her.

Let's restate for emphasis what goes on in Achilles' mind. Deep down, he knows he doesn't control his women, but he does own his sex organ. Its use for temporary dominance of the female sex partner overrides his whole value system. Education and experience outside the underclass supposedly bring some judgment about behavior; nevertheless, this liability is not uncommon among members of all three classes.

Why?

The stereotype of the black family is that of a strong female and a weak male, with the woman as the head of the household. When Bill Cosby's show became the number-one hit series on TV, Bill Cosby would ask his friend Dr. Alvin Pouissant, a professor of psychiatry at Harvard Medical School who specializes in child behavior, to look over the scripts.

Bill Cosby is a comedian who frequently makes fun of himself and puts himself down. In an interview with the *New York Times*, Dr. Pouissant revealed that he suggested that Cosby counteract "the silly-male, strong-female aspects of the Huxtable relationship, which reproduces in a professional context the stereotype of the black welfare family."

Dogs

Of course, not all black men behave in the same way. Those with strong family ties lead normal lives. Still, the black man's behavior usually is stereotyped in the underclass, where men exhibit sexual behavior in a simplistic and basic fashion. Their value systems aren't influenced by the greater society in America. They have little or no contact with other classes.

By holding his crotch, the black man from this class exhibits a body language that reflects his attitude about his life. He feels that what he holds in his hand nobody's got but him, not even the black woman. That's his club, and it's the only thing he has to control and handle her. He believes that if he loses this, he has no other means to make her his woman.

The only problem he has is that it's effective only when he is having sexual intercourse with her. He knows there are spare men and main men who are waiting to replace him to take control. He has seen this all throughout his life, and as a man, he intends for his penis to be king.

Many black men in the underclass have left home and are in the streets by the age of twelve or thirteen. Even those who don't physically leave home until they are sixteen to eighteen often start spending most of their time in the streets by age twelve or thirteen.

They learn the values of the streets. They learn the behavior of a dog. By being reminded by the black women in their lives that they are dogs, they become proud of being as doggish as they can. These mannerisms are a measurement of manhood.

Carl and Sam live in Woodlawn, a very poor section on the South Side of Chicago. Both wear number buttons on their shirts. Carl has a button with a four inscribed on it; Sam has a button with a five on it. When asked what the buttons represent, here are their answers:

"It's the number of kids I got," Sam says. "Around here when you get your woman pregnant, you want everybody to know that you have made a baby."

"Yes," Carl agrees. "I've got four of them and all of them look just like me."

When asked if they are taking care of these kids, Carl quickly responds. "Hey, that ain't my job. I only make them; the women can take care of them."

Sam interrupts. "You know how Boy Scouts have badges, don't you? Well, these are men's badges. It tells you how much of a man we are and it tells our women to chill, you know. They know we got somebody else to be with if they f—— up."

Sam and Carl belong to the segment of black men in the underclass who believe these badges reflect their honor. Are they totally immature? Pause for moment. Here are two teenagers who seek to be cared for, and expect it's women's role to care for them and their babies—just as their mothers took care of them when they were children. To paraphrase Alexander Pope, "As the tree is bent, so does it grow."

The black men in the underclass live in the present, and the only future they have is to pursue women. Since women are the only significant commodity that many of them have, ownership is very important. Current statistics show that close to 80 percent of today's black females are rejecting marriage. A far cry from the 1920s, when 70 percent of young black women got married. Is this drop in marriages due to young women not wanting to get married or does it reflect that young men don't want marriage?

The black man from the knowledge class also wants control. He, however, can rely on money or status to make sure his woman is not dominant. If the woman is not subservient, the man will terminate the relationship quickly. Since he has more women available to him, he is less affected by the breakup of a relationship than an underclass male.

Crazy Behavior

The threat to black family structure by the Achilles neurosis is compounded by an irrational and careless attitude toward the practice of safe sex.

In this epidemic of AIDS, the majority of black men still do not and will not use condoms. Why?

Various reasons and excuses are given for this reckless behavior. Here are a variety of comments from my focus groups:

Some say it's a shibboleth, i.e., a custom handed down from older groups of men to the younger generation, making it a pseudocommandment.

Some black men state emphatically that they can't feel anything using a condom.

Others say they don't believe they are really having sex when using a condom.

A community leader maintained he could accommodate (please) a woman better without a "raincoat."

Some honestly believe they cannot climax using a condom.

Magic Johnson, one of the great basketball players of our decade, contracted AIDS while having unprotected sex with numerous women. All his millions could not prevent it. He was no exception when he stated in *Sports Illustrated* on November 19, 1991, that "I did my best to accommodate as many women as I could, most of them through unprotected sex."

To Achilles, the idea of wearing a condom is seldom considered. It's like an NFL cornerback playing in a Super Bowl game without a helmet. Wearing a condom would destroy the self-esteem and the notion that "he is doing it all by himself."

If his penis is his greatest asset, why should he cover it up? Even Michael Jackson depicts this behavior. In Jackson's video "Black or White," he repeatedly touches his genitals. He repeats that gesture in his act. Jackson did not originate it. Other young blacks have been doing it for a long time.

The message being sent is crystal clear. "Look at me, I've got it, it's bad, and I'm good with it. You don't cover up something like this. You uncover it and advertise it."

It's a frequent discussion among black women to reveal that when making love, most black men need to be told how good they are, how well they perform, and that they are the greatest. It's their identity. It's an attitude that's present in black males of all ages and from all classes. Wilt Chamberlain, who is fifty-seven years old, exemplifies that age is not a factor.

What better evidence is needed to make the point. A superb athlete and an accomplished businessman, he wrote a book and discussed his lifelong sexual activities with thousands of women.

Among the words used on the preceding pages of this chapter are: deviation, neurosis, obsession, compulsion, unreasoning, disaster, liability, irrational, and crazy. Could an objective reviewer of Wilt Chamberlain's book employ these words as well?

CHAPTER

5

Meet Sapphire

An *obsession* with (not just a desire for) material things is one of the predominant characteristics of most black women in America. The reason for this obsession was addressed in the first chapter. One could argue that there are other reasons: insecurity as a result of being financially disadvantaged too long, or a similar attitude that has affected many Americans of the "me" generation, which is "Get all you can while you have the chance." The point remains that a Sapphire woman uses men to "pile up the goodies."

This creates new psychological problems for the black male. In general, black women are better educated with better-paying jobs than the males, so this behavior translates into an economic liability for the black man. The money and gifts the black man gives to women are not tax deductible, refundable, or recoverable, and neither are they an investment. They are gone forever. The black man is bombarded constantly by the black woman with requests.

"I need a dress."

"I need a purse."

"I need a coat."

"I need a pair of shoes."

"I need a necklace."

"I need a ring."

"I need tires for my car."

"I need gas for my car."

"I need medicine."

"I need rent money."

Even if they are just seeing each other socially, it is not unusual for her to ask him for help and assistance. "I need" and "I want" are constantly being programmed into his head.

A black female accountant recently worked out for me the "gimme" economics of this type of life. If he earns $30,000 a year, he will have left about $22,000 after taxes. He is likely to spend or give her $5,000 to $6,000 a year. If she makes $15,000 in salary, she now has an income of $20,000 to $21,000 for the year, of which 25 percent is tax free. His after-tax income is reduced to $16,000 to $17,000 for the year.

But if the salary scales for the genders are reversed, the pressure cooker existence of black males in this situation is horrific.

Then there are some black women who relate to two or three "spare" men. After they get their side money and gifts from these men, plus the money and gifts from their main man, they have almost doubled their economic benefits.

It will come as no surprise that there are also black men who live off women. Disregarding the extremes of this behavior (pimps), this situation has the additional tendency to further erode self-esteem and may lead to alcoholism, arguments, and physical abuse.

Rhonda and Harry

Too many black women do not take proper care of themselves. They are more concerned with their looks, clothes, and instant pleasures than their health. They are more prone to abuse alcohol, sex, and drugs. Often in their twenties, they end up in the hospital clinic or at the doctor's looking for help. Harry and Rhonda's situation illustrates how Rhonda's problems become Harry's expenses.

Even though Rhonda is only twenty-seven, Harry, the man she has been going with for the last four years, is obliged to keep certain medications at his apartment for her. Rhonda has ulcers and has to take two pills a day, each pill costing $1.50. She expects Harry to pay for this $90-a-month prescription, and to keep hay fever medicine, Tylenol, Maalox, hydrogen peroxide, and Preparation H in his medicine cabinet at all times.

Rhonda complains from the time he picks her up until he drops her off the next day. All Harry hears is, "My body aches. Will you please rub me?" or "My ear is driving me crazy," or "My feet hurt." Harry spends about $200 a month on Rhonda's prescription and over-the-counter drugs as well as on her cigarettes.

As Rhonda teaches school and lives with her sister, Harry can only see her weekends. At the end of the weekend, Rhonda picks up all the medications and takes them home with her, only to complain the next weekend that "there's no medicine here for me to take." When he hears this complaint, Harry goes back out to the drugstore and the cycle starts over again.

Rhonda makes Harry financially and medically responsible for everything that she can. Though she takes the medicine from his home, she nevertheless expects him to always have a supply for her. She never offers to pay for any items that she complains are missing from his medicine cabinet. Although Harry doesn't smoke, he is expected to keep a supply of cigarettes at his home, which she often takes with her when she leaves.

It has never dawned on Harry that she has a great medical plan at school, and while he pays for her medication, she gets the refunds.

Harry is sure of one thing: if he does not take her to the doctor or, preferably, give her money for a visit, she will surely say she is too ill to have sex with him.

The Angry Captain

For the black man married to a black woman, the economic liabilities can be disproportionately greater than for the single black man. The Case of the Angry Captain is a prime example.

Charles was an Army captain with a wife of fourteen years. She decided that with two young daughters, she did not want to travel from army base to army base any longer. She insisted that Charles get out of the service and return to Chicago.

Charles pointed out that he had only six more years to go before he could take early retirement, probably with a higher rank, which would have given him greater retirement income. His wife was adamant. If she left without him, he would have to support two domiciles. To save his marriage, he resigned his commission.

Charles regrets it. "I'm in the Reserves now, and the young men that I trained have passed me in rank and now I have to say 'Sir' to them."

Charles formed his own construction company, which he has been operating for ten years. Charles says, "I'm downright upset at my wife and my two daughters, who are just like her. Most of the time they don't even know I'm around. The only time they look for me is to ask me for money. As soon as they get it, I am forgotten. Would you believe that most of the time I have to prepare my own meals at home? An elephant pays more attention to a gnat on his rump than my wife and daughters pay to me."

He stays away from home as much as possible because "All I see are medical bills, school bills, car bills, clothing bills, and more clothing bills." He angrily adds, "My problem is this woman I married twenty-four years ago. All she did for me was produce two clones of herself. If I earned three times as much as I do now, they would spend it all."

"This Marriage Is Killing Me"

Note that Charles complains about his daughters, as well as his wife. The Sapphire behavior is learned and passed on to another generation. Many black men endure "I need," "I want," and "Gimme" from women outside his immediate family: his mother-in-law and her mother, or his wife's sisters and aunts. The Case of Mama Too illustrates this dilemma.

At another focus group, one of the participants was Marvin, a thirty-year-old pharmaceutical salesman, who described his life.

"I was real successful in the business," he began. "I had received the top sales award in my region for two years straight, purchased a nice home in Webster Grove, a suburb of St. Louis, and gotten engaged to Ruth, a schoolteacher in the city.

"We made our plans for the first five years of marriage, which was to save enough so we could start a family, when she'd be thirty-two and I'd be thirty-five. By then, I expected to have made some investments and she could take a sabbatical for a couple of years.

"Everything went fine until we got married, and then Ruth and her mother started playing games. First, Ruth had to send her mother money each month. It started out with a hundred dollars. She said her mother was having difficulty managing her bills, that her electricity and gas had gone up. I could understand that, so I agreed.

"Then, a few months later, she was sending her two hundred dollars a month because she said her mother's telephone bill was high since she lived in the city and had to call us out in the suburbs. I told her they should quit spending so much time on the phone, but she didn't pay any attention to that. I reminded her that this was money that was to be put away for our five-year plan.

"At the beginning of our second year of marriage, her

mother 'suddenly' lost her lease after being there for twelve years. Guess where she wanted to move? 'Love me, move my mother,' Ruth said. I told her with all due respect, 'I'm not sleeping with your mother. My marriage contract was with you, not your mama.'

"Well, for the next three months the dishes weren't washed, meals were seldom cooked, and the house was never cleaned. When I would complain, she quickly reminded me we wouldn't have these problems if her mother was there to help her.

"In a huff, I'd cut the grass on Saturday and wash the cars, and when I went back in the house, nothing had been touched. She spent more and more time in the city at her mother's, telling me that if her mother and grandmother lived with us she could spend more time at home with me. She also quit her job.

"By the end of our second year, when she rationed our sex life to once a week, my sales were off forty percent and I had lost twenty-three pounds. I had to have all my suits taken in and the doctor had me on medication for my nerves.

"The next pressure began building when shopping bills started coming in and all her fifteen credit cards were charged to their limits.

"Ruth said that her mother and grandmother were so depressed at times that she took them shopping. She always liked to pick something up for them since they couldn't afford anything for themselves.

"In July of our third year of marriage, I threw in the towel and agreed for her mother and grandmother to move into our house in the two rooms set aside for our

future children. By then, I was ready to try anything just
to get some peace of mind.

"By now, I had been transferred to a different territory
because my sales were low. I had to travel farther away
from home and therefore got home later at night, so Ruth
and I weren't spending much time together. By giving in,
I thought we might spend more time together.

"That was a big mistake. I won't even try to describe
how they ran me crazy. Half the time, they were planning
changes in the house without consulting me. The house
was only four years old and they completely redecorated
it—with my money. Any lovemaking, what there was of
it, was now once or twice a month and had to take place
on Wednesday night, when her mother and grandmother
would go to church prayer meeting and it had to end
before they got back.

"Sometimes I would come home and Ruth's mother
would tell me Ruth had gone back into the city to visit a
girlfriend. It got so I didn't care if they were telling the
truth or lying. I've just seen a lawyer because this marriage is killing me."

Not Isolated Incidents

Black Americans will recognize the situations described in
this and the previous chapters. Most will admit that they
are not isolated instances. While they may not acknowledge that they have shared these experiences, they can
relate to other similar stories.

In physics, there is a law of diminishing returns, i.e.,

drop a ball and it will bounce up halfway, on the second bounce, it will bounce half of the second bounce—and continue until the bounce is gone.

When all the positive aspects of a healthy black family life start eroding until there is less and less life in the family, healthy black families will disappear.

Because black men have begun to lose self-esteem and confidence as women took over the roles as the head of the family, it began to destroy the family. It's not that the black women were doing a bad job raising children, but it sent mixed signals to the young. Soon the stereotype of the black family became the norm.

Until African-Americans understand what is happening, and both genders realize what they are doing to black life in America, their futures are bleak. Because many black men treat women like barter, and the women respond as bartered goods, black America is stymied.

Until black Americans no longer condone such circumstances in their own families and demand a different behavior based on more enduring values, there will be no progress in the march for black advancement.

6

Bending the Twig

In the African-American underclass, almost 80 percent of the households are run by single parents, and most of those single parents are women. The head of household may be the mother, the grandmother, or even the grandmother whose main priorities *do not include the development of their children*. This does not mean that they do not love their children; obviously, most do. With the absence of a dependable and reliable man from the relationship, her other needs take on a higher priority. She focuses on these higher-priority needs at the expense of the child's development.

Listen to a Chicago judge relate two recent experiences:

"Last year, a female elementary school principal phoned me and asked if I would get a couple of my friends to come to the school and show some of the young boys how to use the bathroom properly. She said they were sitting on the toilet to urinate. Can you believe that? When we got there, sure enough, half of these little guys would go to the boys' washroom and squat on the toilet like a woman.

"Several of the boys told me that's how they do it at home. It's a shame these women are unable to show them the basic difference. In the second place, I don't understand why the women are squatting in front of their children.

"Recently, I had a case before me where the father is petitioning to get custody of his seven-year-old son, who is now staying with his ex-wife on the West Side. It appears that the little boy has been sexually abused. According to the father, the boy was staying overnight with him during a visit and crawled into bed with his dad and tried to give him oral sex.

"There is nothing natural about that, and if the father's description is accurate, his ex-wife and her boyfriend should be put away for as long as the law allows. There is something wrong and there's no excuse for it. Where do you think these little boys are going to be ten or fifteen years from now?"

The judge's description of little boys sitting on the toilet to urinate depicts the level and condition of many young males coming out of the home environment into the schools. Not only do they have an identity crisis, *they also have a total developmental and survival crisis*. If they have been observing their mothers' and other females' behavior in the bathroom, what have they been observing in the bedroom? What have they overheard in conversations in the home, and what mental imprinting has occurred in their young, impressionable minds?

Millions of dollars and countless investigative hours have already been spent exploring the breakdown of the black American family. Millions of dollars and countless hours have been spent on working out solutions to halt this disintegration.

Nothing has worked. *Nothing will work until black men and women of all classes admit to the destructive dynamics of many female-headed households.* The women who head these homes are neither encouraged nor inclined to change the dynamics. Not many will face the fact that our young men, without fathers living at home, are getting shortchanged by growing up without male supervision and a father who sets an example. They'll find plenty of street men willing to fill this need, and often it's the wrong kind of fulfillment.

In human development, by age five, the basic personality of the child is developed. The "id," the instinctual impulses that lead to immediate gratification of primitive needs, is well developed. The "ego," the "I" or individual as distinguished from other, is also well developed. The least developed, the "superego," that which reflects the parental standards, is well developed by the time the child enters the school classroom.

In the majority of black households, the women have total control over these early years during the child's personality development. The way the child sees himself or herself is clearly a result of how the parental figure, the black woman, has controlled, treated, and guided the child during those years. The standards that mold the child's superego are the standards taught by the black mother as the child is rewarded, and encouraged.

Here is what Lee and Thelma, first- and third-grade

teachers in an inner-city school in Chicago, have to say about the black children in today's classrooms.

"I've been teaching for twenty-two years, and I've seen the changes in these children," Lee says. "The little girls are fast these days, just like their mamas.

"I had one last year come to school with bleached blond hair who told me her mother did it with dye left over after she did hers. Other little girls come to school with play makeup in their purse and some even have nerve to try to wear it in school."

"Yes, that is the truth," Thelma interrupts. "I make them remove it in my class. But do you know I had a mother threaten me because I washed the lipstick and makeup off of her daughter's face?

"There were two girls in my class this year carrying tampons in their purses. When I asked them what it was for, they told me that when they get cursed, they were going to use them like their mamas. This is just third grade. These little girls have just seen too much for their own good."

"The little boys don't even have to be sexually aggressive," Lee says. "Some of the little girls go around pulling their little dresses up and making all kinds of dirty remarks like 'You can't have this' or 'Come get this.' "

"That's mild," Thelma adds. "I intercepted a note from one of my third-grade girls to a boy that said, 'You lic my pusy and I lic you dic.' I went out of my way to go by the mother's house that evening to show her the note. When the mother let me in, she and her girlfriend were listening to a song by this group called Bitches With Problems. No wonder her daughter could think of writing such a note."

"The little boys are just as bad. They can repeat this rap crap even before they can spell their names," Lee says. "A lot of them now think they are little studs."

"Mind you, not all of them act this way, but a lot of them do," Thelma says. "We have to spend much of our teaching time handling behavior problems. It leaves a lot less time to teach school subjects."

"The good students really get shortchanged," Lee points out. "By the time you get through teaching them what their mamas should have taught them, the school day is over and the well-behaved children haven't received any attention."

"The language of some of these little boys is just too much to cope with," Thelma says. "This is my twenty-sixth year teaching elementary school, and nineteen years have been with third-graders. I try hard, but the boys today don't show you any respect. They will call you any name they can think of when you stop them from acting out. They'll roll their eyes at you, and give you the finger. Some told me what their mama would do to me," Thelma says.

Lee added, "One big difference today in these boys is they're much more angry than they used to be. I don't know, maybe it is because the mothers resent the little boys more than the little girls. Maybe it's because of their fathers, but I do know the little boys are angrier now.

"I used to spend time after class with those boys who acted this way, but it didn't do any good. Now I send them to the principal's office or to one of the male teacher's rooms until they settle down."

"When the mothers come to school, I can tell immediately where the problem is," Thelma states. "They don't come to see about the child. They just want to make sure the boy is not being sent home for them to deal with."

"That happens often," Lee confirms. "I've had parents tell their children in front of me that they didn't have time for them at home, that they belonged in school, not running around town with their mamas. Many mothers see the school as a baby-sitting service. It gives them time to be free of the child.

"Most little boys don't know how to handle this rejection. I believe they're hungry for their mothers' attention even when the mothers are not around. They know full well we're going to contact their mothers and have them come to the school, so they act up just so it will happen."

"When I first started teaching, there was a lot of concern by parents. Usually, when the child got in trouble, especially the boy, both parents became involved and showed a lot of concern. Now there is usually only the mother or grandmother. Yes, some of them honest to God try to help the kids, but many are upset just because they have to come to school," Thelma points out. "The ones that are cooperative are a pleasure to work with, but they are getting fewer and fewer all the time."

Lee and Thelma are true professionals who see the results of early experiences upon the black child as the child leaves the home environment and enters the school system. They're frustrated that they have to focus on child survival rather than child development. Trying to help the child remain a child has become the central focus in their educational program.

Like a twig, the young child is bent and twisted by the pressures of the home environment. They can't grow straight and healthy, nor can they have a decent adult life, because their early years have decided their fate.

All the Wrong Lessons

Little Donald is enjoying a video cartoon when his mother rushes into the house and tells him to go to his room. He protests, but can tell by her voice that she is angry. He gets up from the living room floor and goes to his bedroom.

Just as he is about to close the door, she hurries into his room carrying the VCR and slips it under his bed. "Now don't you touch it," she says.

He hears his grandmother talking to a man in the living room as his mother leaves him to join her own mother. "I told you the damn thing broke and I threw it out," he hears his mother say.

"I want my VCR," the man responds. "I lent it to you because you said we could watch movies over here sometimes. Now you don't want me in your house. So give it back to me."

The grandmother finally convinces the man that the

VCR is not there. After some more shouting, the man leaves.

His mother comes back into his room and tells Donald, "Leave that set under your bed tonight. You can look at it tomorrow after school."

That evening at dinner, he listens as his aunt, grandmother, and mother discuss how cheap the man is: "You did right, girl," his aunt says to his mother. "I wouldn't have given it back to him, either. You've been spending time with him and just because you don't want him anymore, he wants to take back a gift he gave you. Girl, that man is cheap. You earned that VCR!"

In another case, Felton is working on his third-grade homework assignment in the living room, next to the kitchen. His mother and her two girlfriends are playing cards on the kitchen table. George, his mother's male friend, is about to leave. Felton hears his mother say, "Honey, I'll be waiting tonight when you get off from work. And quit worrying about the Cadillac that was parked out front last night; I told you that was my sister's new friend." George smiles and kisses her good-bye, then he leaves.

"Girl, who was that hunk you had here last night?" one of her girlfriends asks.

"That's Frank," the mother replies. "He thinks he's hot shit because he drives a Cadillac and has a good job. But he's the cheapest man I been out with all year. If he don't start taking care of me, he won't be coming around no more."

"Well, he might be cheap but he looks well hung," the second girlfriend notes. "I know you're being taken care of there."

The mother shrugs her shoulders and says, "He's like a lot of black studs. All he wants is lipstick on his dipstick. I make him think he's real good and it's over with in ten minutes."

"Make him pay, girl. Make him pay. What are you going to do about George? He finds out about Frank, no telling what he'll do," the second girlfriend says.

The mother looks toward the living room and whispers, "I told both of them to park their rides on a backstreet from now on and not to come over before they call. I got the boy to worry about."

Felton hears all of this with the possible exception of his mother's last whispered statement. He's seen both men in the house, sometimes on the same day, and he's seen his mother show equal affection to both. She has ordered him not to mention Frank to George and George to Frank. His mother explains to him that it's nobody's business, and he knows what she means when she tells him, "I'll knock you into next week if you do."

These incidents describe two problems. One, are these isolated occurrences? Two, what are Donald and Felton learning about relationships between the sexes? About honesty? About lying?

Havens of Deceit

Households like Donald's and Felton's are havens of deceit. The mother, aunts, girlfriends, and maybe grandmother are constantly letting a variety of men come and go, drop off gifts or money, have sex, drink, and, frequently, fight. There is one crisis after another, with the crises centered around using, exploiting, manipulating, and controlling the man of the moment.

Day in and day out, month after month, going on sometimes for years, black children see these crises played out. On one side of the coin, the boy soon learns that to be a man means giving women money and having arguments. For the young girl, it's teaching her a pattern of behavior from her role model, which is to learn how to dominate, manipulate, and control the opposite sex.

The boy learns that to be a man usually means no housework, no responsibilities, no pride, no self-respect, and no real love and affection. The black women in the household will spoil the boy, but they will never train him as they do their daughters. When training the black female child, the black woman's focus is on how to bait the black male, how to get him, control him, and finally dominate him. Even in this scenario, the black male child usually serves as an example to prove the mother's lessons to his sisters. Mother may instruct his sisters how to wash his clothes, iron his shirts, and use him every which way as a test model for their future roles as women.

A Blank Slate

Like all newborn babies, the black child is a blank slate that life experiences soon begin to write on. Black women are in charge of almost all of his experiences. They have to be. They're the only ones around. When he is a child, the woman determines when he sleeps, eats, looks at television, plays, and when he gets rewarded and punished. She is his primary teacher about the world around him, nevertheless, no matter how caring and loving she is, she can only show the child the world through a woman's eyes.

She cannot teach him what a black man is or how to be a black man. How can she? She is not a black man; consequently, she cannot be a role model.

This is described by Doris, a public health nurse, and Sharon, a social worker, who live in separate cities in the Midwest but teamed up together in a focus group.

Doris points out, "I've been in nursing for twenty-eight years and conditions have gotten worse. More and more young black women are having babies today out of wedlock. Their reasons are quite selfish. They want to have something of their own to love. They're not really concerned about spending quality time with the children or raising them or teaching them."

"Pardon me," Sharon interrupts. "Doris is putting it very nicely. The ones I see here in my city fall into three categories. They either drag the children every place they go, even late at night, or they leave them shut up alone in the apartment by themselves to do whatever they want. Either way, they don't give their kids any personal attention.

"Another way they handle these babies is to just drop them off somewhere, either at their grandmother's or aunt's or even at one of their girlfriends' houses. I've had many of my patients admit that they have babies because they want somebody who will give them honest affection. The man won't, so they have a baby who will."

"I have to agree," Doris adds. "In the last five or ten years, grandmothers are younger than they have ever been, but it's usually only the older grandmothers who end up raising the children. Some mothers even take off and desert their kids. The little baby boys are pathetic. They don't know whether they are going or coming. The mothers get bored easily. They don't play games with these children. They don't read to them [or they can't read]. Those mothers that don't drop the children off with relatives use TV as the around-the-clock baby-sitter and will let them look at anything on TV."

"That's not the worst of it," Sharon says. "Some of these younger mothers seem to want to punish the boys for being like their fathers. More than once I've heard them accuse the little boy and tell him he is going to be a dick dipper just like his father."

"That's nothing," Doris adds. "I've heard two mothers tell their daughters they should get themselves white boyfriends and leave the black ones alone, because the white men know how to treat you and the black men don't. While they were talking, three little black boys were running around the kitchen, hearing everything they said. There is a war out there between the black woman and the black man and the real casualties are the children.

"The black women cannot be blamed for an ongoing situation that has trapped them. And how can they be expected to show black male children how to grow into responsible black men?"

Mother's Confession

The black male's insecurity is deepened even more by the fact that his mother, grandmother, and aunts aren't inclined to promote him as they do the black female child. And if he acts like, looks like, or shows any resemblance to his father, it is thrown up to him and he develops additional insecurities from the fear that he, like his father, will lose her or, even worse, she will get rid of him.

It's from her that he innately learns to be weak, because to be strong means to be gone. Meanwhile, he sees and hears her dish out insults to her current man or hears her tell her girlfriends on the phone how she "punished" her man and everything else she's going to do with him.

The black male child sees these activities and hears these remarks and very early on concludes that all men are dogs, as his mother, grandmother, and aunts often say. "I am a little man," the child thinks, "therefore, I am a little dog and no good." When he hears the most important women in his life talk down to their men even after they have received gifts, he gets mixed signals about being a male.

"Girl, this man is cheap. He brought this dress up here last night thinking he was going to get some of my stuff and I just told him he's gotta do better than that. I need shoes to wear with the dress before he can see me in this outfit, and he's got to take me to get them."

Since the black male child is constantly bombarded with this deprecating type of input, he will be confused about the male role. He absorbs the beliefs that he is supposed to be weak, have no discipline, and rely on women to be dominant and make decisions for him when he grows up. Indirectly, he is "taught" to be a fool even when it goes against his natural instincts. He is taught to disrespect himself and black women in general. Thus, the stereotype is reinforced and becomes fact.

The young child also learns that he is often manipulated in such a way as to get money for his mama. Some days, he may be wearing sneakers bought by Tom, pants bought by Dick, and underwear bought by Harry, something he is acutely aware of. He learns not to have any respect for himself, or for Tom, Dick, or Harry, and is afraid of black women. The black child's expectations that he must pay for sex are constantly reinforced.

The black mother is quick to remind him that "men don't do anything for you, so when they want special treatment, you have to make them buy you things." This is usually part of what is called "the poor mother's confession." She is using "her" weapon just as the man uses "his."

"I only take this treatment from 'him' because I love you. I clean and work so hard just so you can have a decent place to stay and food to eat. But he [either the husband or main man] doesn't care what happens to us. He doesn't give me enough money and I have to force him to take care of his responsibilities. If it wasn't for me, you wouldn't have the things you have right now."

She cries, and naturally the male child tries to hold her and comfort her, so she gets comfort from the black male child, something she is constantly looking for, which is another form of manipulation. Since she can't do it with the father, out of frustration or anger, she does it with the child.

If there is no father in the household, the poor mother's confession to her son is, "I only let that bastard treat me like this 'cause we need some things around here. I'm so tired of his shit. If I didn't have you, I'd find somebody better out there who wants a good woman and who would love me. Just 'cause I got you, that shiftless man thinks I'm here at his beck and call. Men just ain't no good."

It is through this type of behavior that the black male child learns unconsciously, if not consciously, that he is a burden. What child can go through this and escape un-wounded?

The young black female child will get phase two of the poor mother's confession. The black woman will take the adolescent female aside and teach her how to handle this ungrateful, no good, unreliable, and undependable poor excuse for a man. She will teach the child to study the man and observe what he has bought for himself recently, saying something to the effect, "If he comes in here with a new hat, coat, shoes, or anything, you ask him if it's new. If it is, then you ask him where is yours or say how come you didn't get me anything. You have to act real angry and be real quiet for a few days afterward, so he will buy you something. If he doesn't, then you wear something new and let him wonder who gave it to you. He'll give you something then."

Schoolroom and School Yard

When the black male child from the underclass enters school, he enters another female-dominated environ-ment. The only men he sees may be the janitors. In rare cases, there are male principals and one or two male teachers.

Howard, who is a principal of an elementary school in a midsized city in Indiana, describes his experience in to-day's schools.

"I don't want to name my school because I'm part of the administration," he begins. "And when you're part of the administration and you criticize the system, your career is shortened. But, to tell you the truth, it sucks. This is an impossible situation. I have one male teacher and he is a substitute. All of the rest are women, most of whom are black. The unfortunate thing is that many of the teachers are overworked, dissatisfied, and have too many children in their classrooms.

"Most of the children who come here have to be de-programmed if they're ever going to learn anything. Kids coming to first grade can repeat this rap stuff better than they can repeat the Pledge of Allegiance.

"I've got little boys standing on the playground repeating a rap song by Niggers With Attitudes and little girls countering with a song by Bitches With Problems. These are first-, second-, and third-graders. I've got teachers telling little boys that they are little men and they are supposed to behave themselves and I've got other teachers in the teachers' lounge referring to some of these kids as little studs.

"Black male children coming into our classrooms rarely get any personal attention. I have some class sizes as large as thirty-eight pupils in a room with half as many books and supplies as needed, although the parents are charged a book fee.

"I've got parents, mostly mothers, who show up at school to protest because their child was sent home for disciplinary reasons or because they were ill. Many of these mothers are upset because the child's presence at home has interfered with their plans. I've been threatened by mothers and even hit by one for telling her the truth.

"From the top down, this school is falling apart. We have had three general superintendents over the last six years, and conditions are getting worse. Black boys are at the bottom of the totem pole. They enter the system prepared to be unprepared."

Uninformed and Unaware

How is it possible for a black male to develop into a respectable, responsible, and positive adult within these home and school environments?

As the black male child ascends to early teens, he rarely gets any encouragement to study from hassled teachers who spend too much time on repairing the community's social ills, which in turn affects their abilities as teachers.

The males the young men meet are those who date the mothers or aunts. Some of the men look dignified and drive fancy cars, others look unkempt, while still others may look like black men dressed in white men's clothes; no matter what they look like, they never talk with the young boys. They never explain what it is like to be a black man and what it is like to be involved with his mama. One or two men might go through the motions of accepting him as a little friend, but most black men will simply tolerate his presence because they went through the same maturing process and can't readily recognize it as a problem.

It is apparent that there's a need for *intensive* yet positive black male involvement in the development of black boys. Millions of black American males enter adolescence unprepared for *life*. They are uninformed and unaware about any of the enduring values. They become the stock players in Sapphire's "real deal."

The unmarried or divorced young woman with two or three children by different men is herself looking for love and attention in the best way she can. But she, too, is trapped in the system that causes the situation to spiral downward.

The Real Deal

When the black youth forms his first relationship with a black girl, their different agendas are already set. Hers has been formed by the older females in her household. She expects to finish high school and probably go on to college—unless she gets pregnant. His is based on an adolescent, macho attitude learned on the street, not by guidance or discipline. This first "encounter" is usually short-lived.

Both soon move on to the next level, the female-dominated and male-submissive relationship. This is when the young man learns the "real deal." All of a sudden, he becomes a main man or one of the spare men. He becomes the man who visits the woman in her home, who drives her around in his car, and who gives her gifts. He has become a clone of the men he observed at home throughout his childhood years. He has come to accept his role.

Most of the black women he meets have different faces. He finds that some are promiscuous and expect gifts and money. Many are not promiscuous and are strong-minded enough to decide that education is their highest priority, though marriage is not for them. They may use men for their own agenda, i.e., the need for companionship, love, and having a relationship that is normal.

For his part, the picture he sees of himself may seem normal to him, but is not normal psychologically or emotionally. He may have several girls (ranging from the promiscuous to the virtuous), and each girl may have one or more male friends. That he is obliged to please one or more with gifts constantly, that is expected, but he does not feel misused until matters get out of hand; or one of the girls has an unplanned pregnancy.

Another part of the problem for black girls is that birth control has been damned by many black ministers who claim the Pill and other birth control methods are black genocide. So the girls, even the best and the brightest, seldom use contraception. As the surgeon general of the United States, Dr. Joycelyn Elders, pointed out in a *New York Times* interview on January 30, 1994, referring to unplanned pregnancies, "I began to realize how much they [young black women] had been exploited by the religious right but also by their own kind with this talk of contraception being genocide."

So with young girls advised against using contraceptives, and young boys thinking it is unmanly to use them, the cries of newborn babies are not cries of joy.

Only when the pain finally penetrates the young black man's mind is he aware of the missing parts to this jigsaw puzzle. It is often too much for him to bear. He wards off these painful feelings by either denying them entirely or blocking them out of his conscious mind.

The Black Man's Journey

For the emotionally deprived black man, he is constantly roaming and searching for affirmation of his identity and his "manhood." For the underclass and some of the labor class, their environment doesn't permit them the option to build, create, and produce strong financial assets. For these black men, then, their manhood becomes defined by sexual relations with women. They begin the journey of searching for women, each one hoping to discover the one who will crown his manhood.

His search takes him through beauty salons, dance clubs, neighborhood lounges, and even churches. These places permeate black communities. They are the black communities' most successful enterprises. This is where the women are.

The black nightclubs and small lounges today are primarily the places where many black men go to meet black women—hopefully, to sleep with. Since he knows that nine out of ten women are there to find a man, he travels from club to club, always hoping to meet someone. Wednesday night, Friday night, and Saturday night are beef market nights in the black clubs and lounges.

A young woman and man, Geri and Leroy, describe what goes on in the Case of We Protect Each Other.

Leroy talks first. "Man, black people are out at these nightclubs just plain looking. Geri and I are just real good friends, so we hang out together. That way, I can protect her if she doesn't want to talk to a certain guy and she's my excuse if I don't want to talk to a certain sister," Leroy explains. "Each sister is out there to pick up a man if she can."

"Most of them will tell you they're not out there for that," Geri interjects, "but I know better. Girlfriends always talk about going out looking for a man, but when a man asks them about it, they never admit it. I suggested to Leroy one time that we start a club and call it the One Night Stand. I bet we would be successful because that's what it's all about. I mean sex for one night with no long relationship or commitment."

"Yeah," Leroy agrees. "When I walk through a typical black club, I know there are five women out of every ten who will leave with me if I look like I'll give them money—and I'm just a regular-looking guy. If I bring up the topic of cocaine and say I got some, it makes a pickup that much easier."

"Let's face it," Geri says, "most of us know we can find men there who want to go to bed with us. But we aren't going to turn down any presents or money. We all need things.

"When Leroy and I are out, I'll give him a signal if the guy I'm talking to is someone I might like to get to know. Then Leroy will move out of the way to the other side of the club. If I give him a different sign that I don't want to talk to this brother, Leroy will interrupt the conversation and start talking with me."

"Any sisters I meet in a club are only interested in one night. If it works out, the affair may go on for a week or a month or a year. In two hours, we can go through four clubs. If we haven't found soulmates before the third club, something is wrong. I always give my number to at least three or four women before I get to the fourth club. They won't give me their numbers but most will call me, sometimes as soon as the next day," Leroy says.

"Let me say it politely," Geri summarizes. "When women tell you they are not there to get f——ed, they're lying. There's an old axiom that says, 'Nobody goes to a bar to get married.' They'll lie and pretend they are there to party, but that's all a front and there is no doubt about it."

As the black man travels from club to club, he learns that if he is to get a black woman, he has to be chosen, and that means getting her attention. If he wears a small gold spoon or razor blade on a gold chain around his neck, he will have his choice, although the women still really do the initial choosing. The symbols tell the women that he is into cocaine or drugs. Leroy pointed out, a good number of the women in the clubs are into coke and other drugs. They will gladly become friendly and leave with a black man who gets their attention with the spoon or razor.

Harry, a postal worker in Chicago, says, "I can't afford dope money, but I'm going to have to find a way to find some because all the finer women will only leave with you if you got some cocaine. Even the ugly ones try to hold out on you if you don't have some 'caine.'" Or as another black man states, "I can't get any from the sister unless I get some crack or money or something for her."

Although Leroy is heterosexual and accompanies Geri as a friend, some black women prefer a male homosexual as an escort. Some say that at some point, a male heterosexual will often target in on them as a sexual mate after an evening's frustrating search. Another reason is that the conversation by the homosexual male, who usually is extremely obvious in his sexual preference, can be very entertaining to the woman who is sitting waiting to be approached. Still another reason given by some black women for preferring the homosexual male's protective company is that gay men can usually identify other male homosexuals and alert them.

Another trick in the beef market is for the black man to hold his car key chain in his hand so the woman can read the symbol on it. If it's a BMW, Mercedes, Lincoln, or any other luxury car, it immediately stimulates interest. When he wants more of her attention, he can offer to buy her a split of champagne or an expensive whiskey just to convince her that he can afford her.

Once this is established, he is chosen, at least for the evening. If he isn't chosen, he moves on to the next available woman and works his way down to the less attractive ones and finally to the older women in the clubs. Warren, who has owned several clubs, describes the musical chairs game played in nightclubs.

"I've owned clubs for the last thirty years. Before that, I managed a couple of them in New York. Clubs are different now. In New York, they are more integrated than in

Chicago, except in Harlem," Warren says. "When I say 'integrated,' I don't just mean black and white, but also older people and younger people. That's not as true in Chi Town. A lot of clubs in New York have restaurants attached to them, but not in Chicago.

"Here on the South Side, there is very little integration. You very seldom find a white guy in my clubs nowadays. Every now and then, you might find one or two white chicks, but they will always be with a black dude.

"It used to be that you had to have good entertainment and good music and everybody loved dancing. You sold a lot of liquor because everyone was thirsty from all the dancing and jumping around. Not anymore.

"Drinking is down a great deal in the last few years. The younger crowd, up to age twenty-five, don't buy women drinks that much and there is more bar sitting and conversations in the club.

"I think the women are different, too. It used to be that very few women would come in the club unescorted, but now most of them come by themselves or with their girlfriends. I owned a club once where the bar was right in the front window, and I used to tell my bartender to give the first two drinks free to any woman who sat at the bar. Men passing by would see them and come in to buy a drink just to talk with them.

"I don't have to do that today because there's a shortage of black men. There are women all over the place in my clubs. One of my places will accommodate about eight hundred people, and there are always twice as many women as men. I personally don't play around in my clubs; I've kind of got my own private stock of women and I don't allow them to go out clubbing.

"My reason is because most of the women in the clubs today are low-class. They are a different quality of woman than the sixties and seventies," Warren admits. "Most of the guys will go from one chick to the next until he finds one that he thinks he can sleep with for a night or two. If he can't find a cute young one, he will usually settle for an ugly one; it doesn't really matter. There's an old saying, 'The more you drink, the prettier she gets,' and, besides, if you get a good ugly one, she'll be so grateful she won't run around on you as much as a pretty one," he jokes.

"I feel for the young black dudes today. These women in the bars today are like the old slave markets. The best-looking ones go to the highest bidder. Now there are many upscale clubs, attracting the better-educated and well-heeled men and women. Everything may seem genteel, but they're still looking for sex and satisfaction.

"Now I would never say it in the public because I make my living from them, but it's true. With most of the women in my clubs, if you go to their apartments, there's very little furniture, an empty refrigerator, and a closet full of cheap clothes.

"Some guys come to one of my clubs three nights a week. They don't miss a week. They know every time a new woman is in the place and it usually only takes them a couple of nights before one of them takes her to the killing floor at one of the hotels down the street.

"There ain't no courting or dating in the clubs and bars anymore. It's just quick f——ing. It might last for a week or two, then she is off with another dude and he is looking again. But let's face it, it's more fun than picking up whores on the street. Still, the cost is about the same.

"I've got two sons, one is twenty-six and the other is

twenty-eight. Both of them are managers at two of my clubs. They've told me several times that they would rather go through hell than to get serious with any of these women in clubs," Warren concludes.

Churches are also a stop on the black man's journey, although a less frequent one. Eric describes a typical approach.

"I go to church every now and then, but it's usually on big church days like Easter or Christmas. It's easier to find a woman in church, but they are mostly married women. The single ones seem to want a commitment before you ask them out," Eric complained. "Just last month, I met this nice woman at my Baptist Church. She sang solo in the choir, and after church I went downstairs to their refreshment table where they mingle. I started a conversation with her and ended up seeing her the next week.

"When I went over to see her, she takes out this scrapbook and shows me pictures of her when she was twenty. She liked to talk and complain and she looked ten times better at forty than at twenty, still, I decided not to hit on her. It wasn't just her looks. I could sense she was going to be possessive and complaining about everything all the time," he said. "So I made a lot of small talk and I left.

"You know what she did? She called me up the next month and accused me of not asking her out again because I didn't get any. I tried to explain to her that I didn't expect to sleep with her, but she didn't want to believe me. She said, 'I taught you a lesson because you thought I was going to be an easy lay, but I showed you, didn't I?' " Eric quoted her.

"Hell, I never laid a hand on her. She is just a typical tired broad. Most of them at these churches are that way.

Men stopped wanting them, so they go to church for Jesus Christ to be their main man and if it ain't Jesus, it's the minister. Some of them hit on women in their congregation," Eric explains. "I think that's why more black men don't take the church seriously.

"I know this one Apostle Church where they have over three thousand members, yet there aren't over two hundred men. There are a lot more women in all these black churches today than there are men. That's another reason it's so easy to pick women there."

The congregations of black churches have few single women between the ages of eighteen and thirty-five. Consequently, most of the congregations are composed of very young females who are under twelve or thirteen, and females over thirty-five. The age bracket most often sought after by the black man is present in the least numbers in the churches. The few men who attend regularly are older and usually married, and some of them, like the minister, sleep with several women in the congregation, an indictment not made lightly.

Eric implies this in his statement that "most of them hit on women in the congregation." The impact of this practice is one of the main reasons that more black men do not attend or participate in church activities. As one elderly black man said, "Why do I want to go to that church? The first time I went with my wife, the preacher put an over-friendly arm around her. That was the last time I went to church. There ain't no difference in what goes on in the street and what goes on in church."

Except for the black family, the black church has been the main foundation for the protection and advancement of black people in America. Civil rights movements historically have gained acceptance because of the church's participation. Many so-called black leaders have survived and lived longer because they wore the collar of religion. Historically, most white Americans have hesitated to attack this foundation or its figurehead, the minister, and many black Americans see it as their only alternative that will make their lives better "by and by."

In the past, black ministers and religious leaders have performed remarkable service for the black community at large. The sexual misconduct by some has diluted their effectiveness in the movement, as well as any moral suasion in changing Achilles behavior.

Their behavior has created an enormous credibility gap. The actions and behaviors of these ministers have made a mockery of the invitation on Sunday morning for the black man to join the church.

Many black men are bitter. As one young black man stated, "They drive the most expensive cars, wear the best suits and jewelry, and live in a better house than me. It ain't God that's buying this for him, it's those black Baptist women who are doing it." Richard, the speaker, is an articulate, well-educated, forty-three-year-old administrative assistant to a prominent black politician. He explains and makes his point very succinctly in the Case of Chicken and My Mama.

"I stopped going to church as soon as I was big enough to say no. I used to recite Bible verses, sing in the youth choir, and once even presented a sermon. But I never liked the way the preacher did us. After church services, he would come to our house Sunday afternoon and stay for dinner. We kids dared not eat until after he had filled his plate. He was like a pig. He would always take the best part of the chicken and my brothers and sisters and I would get what was left. Then we had to go outside and play while he talked to Mama.

"We knew he was messing with Mama because three or four times my sister found his handkerchief with lipstick all over it in Mama's clothes hamper. I guess he was afraid to take it home because his wife would find it.

"As far as I am concerned, all that most black ministers do is make great speeches to give a lot of false hope to black people. Maybe that helps some of my people, but I don't need it. One thing for sure, they rarely live up to what they preach."

Because a small percentage of ministers abuse their calling, black men resent the fact that they are not answerable to any higher authority. This taint has stained the calling so that many black men see the church as just another beef market with the preacher as "HNIC," head nigger in charge. As a result, those congregations headed by sincere and committed ministers are always suspect and are never considered by the black man as a real source of refuge and growth in character.

How many ministers are the exception to the rule? An indication of the answer to this question can be seen in a letter from one with firsthand experience relating to a minister and his family, in the Case of PK.

Jay has been a PK (a preacher's kid) for forty years, all of his life. He is also the grandson of a preacher, nephew of a preacher, with four generations of ministers in his family.

"To tell the truth, I would never be a minister," Jay says. "There are two types. The sincere, top-level professionals who care and really serve the community; they're underpaid and usually poor and broke all the time, like all my family. Then there are the creative ones who create wealth for themselves at the expense of the community. I never wanted to be poor or broke and I would never consider being a rip-off artist. A preacher was the last thing I wanted to be.

"They can do a lot of good and though I'm not very religious, I do believe in the spirit and in God. I could never be a hypocrite like some of them.

"When I was about eight years old, this black woman came to church one Sunday morning and took me over to the side of the pulpit. She pointed to a brown bag of groceries that she had brought my father. Often parishioners would bring us food, since they didn't put too much money in the collection plate. She looked directly in my eyes and pointed to the bag and said, 'If you don't act nice, I ain't ever gonna bring you and your papa no more food.'

"Well, from that time on, I made up my mind that I would never put myself in a position where I had to rely on women and brown bags in church.

"As far as sexual transgressions, I saw that happening often. Many women who come to church are unmarried, or their husbands deserted them and they're so desperate for male companionship that they become very easy targets for the deacons and minister. I've seen more souls conceived than saved in my lifetime. I've known married deacons who have gotten new members in church pregnant.

"There were elders in my father's church who have been accused of visiting women in their homes a little too regularly while their husbands were at work. I could go on for days and days about things I've seen and know

firsthand what happened. I hate to admit it, but the first
time I had sex, at age sixteen, was in my father's church.
The woman was attractive and twice my age. I thought it
exciting at the time until I learned she had given me a
venereal disease.

"If a man is looking for a woman, the church is the most
likely place to find them, married, single, old, and a few
young ones, who first check you out to see if you come to
church three or four times. Not all churchgoing women
are that way, but there are an awful lot of them like that.

"I'm going to share with you part of a letter that I wrote
to my dad. No one has seen it, not even him, because I'm
not sure how he would take it. He is in his eighties and
retired now and we have had some pretty candid conversations about the church and folks who go there.

" 'Dear Dad,

" 'I want you to know that I love you, respect you, and
look up to you more than any person who has walked this
earth. I am strong and successful because of the sacrifices
you made for me. You never let us go hungry, even when
there was very little in the collection plate. You always
provided and I know you always tried to demonstrate the
way I should live by living that way yourself.

" 'Much of the respect that I have for you stems from
the fact that you have never lied to me, no matter what
the consequences, and this pragmatic part of you makes
me love you even more.

" 'I know it has been hard for you since Mom died
twenty years ago and you have remained a widower to
this day. I have to tell you that last week when you
confessed sleeping with several single women in the past
twenty years, some of whom were in the church congre-

gation, I was shook up. I had to have time to get a new perspective on my idol, my dad. It also made you more human.

" 'I can now truly say you are no less an idol to me now than you were before because I know the good that you have done, the many people you have touched, and the people you have helped spiritually far outweigh the human sexual transgressions that you told me about.' "

With tears silently rolling down his cheeks, Jay folded the letter and put it away.

"The rest is too personal," he said. "My dad was one of the few ministers that I would bet my life on was straight. And he'll always be one of the best ministers I've ever known. He has done so many things and has been written up in the *Congressional Record*."

Jay posed the question: "Ask yourself this, if the best are guilty of such transgressions, what are the majority, who are mediocre, and the worst guilty of? I've seen married district superintendents of the Methodist Church bring their special ladies into town and put them up at one hotel, while they stayed at another hotel with their wives. I've seen preachers smoke dope with women parishioners on Friday night and walk to the pulpit on Sunday morning singing, Holy, Holy, Holy, Lord God Almighty.

"Now, I'm not without sin," Jay exclaims, "but I don't put myself out there as representing God and trying to save anybody's soul, either. I know a congregation where the minister was building a new church with money raised by the congregation. He got married this summer and half his congregation, mostly women, stopped coming to his church. They had to stop building the new church. All these women were upset because he got married. What does that tell you?"

Such soap operas like the ones described by Jay are too often accepted by the community as the norm. As Plautus said about 200 B.C., "Practice what you preach." So when the minister's own Achilles' heels are exposed, it's a turnoff. When the black man encounters this behavior on his odyssey through life, it only reinforces his criteria for measuring manhood.

Another area of discontent involves inhabitants in the underclass public housing. Government's well-meaning projects for the poor are usually instant slums. When his journey brings him into contact with the black woman in the underclass who lives in public housing and/or on welfare, the black man puts himself at risk. Not from her, but from the conditions.

If they connect and he moves in, she retains control of the relationship because she lives there and he doesn't. She lets him stay with her for two reasons. First and foremost, she is frightened and he provides her and her young ones with protection; second, he will add money to the family coffers. Rape and child molestation occur frequently in these developments, and the high numbers reflect only the ones that are reported to the police.

The black woman in public housing seeks out a man who can physically protect her from male predators in the development. Although self-preservation may be the primary reason for keeping the new man around, the black man who tries to develop a romantic relationship with a woman who needs him for protection is either a modern version of Batman or Superman.

Often, there are more fights and shootings in these

environments than in the average community, so he is exposed to life-threatening situations when he remains in this setting. Random nightly shootings and muggings are only part of what he has to accept when picking up or dropping off a woman from this environment.

If he's driving a relatively new car, he dare not leave it unattended. When arriving to pick up his date and when bringing her home, he is unable to see her safely to her door without taking a chance with both his car and his life.

Ralph, a salesman, describes one of these experiences in the Case of Fire at the Door.

"I normally don't talk with women who live in public housing. I'm a salesman and go just about anyplace, but the poorer projects are one of the few places I normally won't go. But I met this real attractive sister who was also very bright. I figured by the way she talked she was exciting so I started dating her. At first, I would meet her at a club where I first met her. We stayed in a hotel a few times. Then I started taking her over to my apartment after I knew I could trust her.

"Well, I started liking her a lot so I made the mistake of trying to visit her at her apartment. She stayed in the Robert Taylor Project here in Chicago. I knew I was in trouble the very first time I went to see her. I mean, the building inside looked bombed out. Only one elevator was working. I was afraid to leave my car on the street but I did.

"To get to her apartment on the ninth floor, I had to walk through a dark entrance. The ride on a urine-smelling elevator and the walk down two smelly stair-wells [the elevator didn't stop on the ninth floor] was unreal. When I got to her apartment, the door looked as if it had been scorched. When I asked her what happened, she said some young kids threw some gasoline on the door and set it on fire.

"She wanted me to stay late with her until she put her three kids to bed. I knew I couldn't stand to be in that kind of place very long. When she asked me if I would help catch the kids who were trying to burn her door, I made up my mind that a relationship with her was crazy. I left and never called her again.

"And, yeah, when I got to my car, the tires were gone, as was my radio. I had to get towed to the car dealer.

"It cost me six hundred dollars for new tires and fifty dollars for the tow, all because I had gotten involved with this woman from the projects. I know it's not her fault. She's trapped there, but it doesn't mean I have to fall into the same trap."

Due to the social mobility of the black women at clubs, churches, lounges, and social gatherings, often those from the lower socioeconomic groups are able to position themselves around black men who are employed. These women may not live in a high-rise building, but rather in scattered apartments throughout the city. When this is the case, it may take the labor- and knowledge-class black men several experiences with these women before they discover their inability to cope with the conditions they encounter. The underclass black men have less choice. They may be living with one woman this year and another one next year in the same housing development.

When the black man thinks he's found that special woman in the projects, he may attempt to take her away from her friends and family, who continually involve themselves in the relationship. This may precipitate moving her and himself across town, out of town, or even out of state. He feels that by getting her away from the people who interfere with their lives, the relationship will work itself out. This usually backfires, since women maintain close home contacts by phone and visits, so the move is often in vain.

Here is the story of Charles, a sergeant who worked as an Army recruiter. He asked for and received a transfer from Illinois to Georgia just so he could take his wife away from her family and friends, who were interfering with their marriage. Here is how he explained it in the Case of Take Her to the Mountaintop.

"I met my wife at a house party when I was on leave in Chicago. We dated for six months before we got married. The first thing I know, her mother and girlfriends were over in our house constantly. They were always drumming something up until I got fed up and put in for a transfer.

"We moved to Georgia in June. Just as we got settled, her mother came to visit in August. That wasn't so bad, but our telephone bill was as much as our monthly food bill. My wife was still having these crazy ideas about hanging out in the street when I wasn't home. I thought about getting an overseas assignment, but I couldn't swing it.

"She got a whole set of new girlfriends and started acting wild until I couldn't take it any longer. I went to see the chaplain and he told me several things. First, that you can take the girl out of the projects, but you can't take the projects out of the girl. Second, he told me to try and get counseling for both of us. My wife refused to go, said she was having too good a time. I went, and after a dozen sessions, I realized I couldn't change things. I love her, but right now I'm living on the base and I just want out."

Behavioral changes are just as difficult for blacks as for whites and other groups. The patterns of behavior are set, and unless the woman or the man understands and is willing to accept change, it is difficult to change. Humans, after all, are creatures of habit.

The journeys taken by most black men never get them to a haven of peace of mind, contentment, and some happiness. Black women have less opportunities to travel and are more often tied to the mother in a friend-to-friend relationship rather than a mother-daughter relationship.

The luckier black men are the ones with upward mobility. They reach the knowledge class and may go through several changes before settling down into more permanent relationships. Only then do they realize that on earth, there is no Shangri-la at the end of a treadmill. They step off and find their way.

The Black Man's Haven

More and more black men in the knowledge class are becoming aware that since the breakdown of the African-American family, "love" has little to do with genuine affection and even less to do with a feeling of warm personal attachment. Circumstances that create friction between the genders have surged beyond control and have tied black life into a Gordian knot that is nearly impossible to unravel.

This has caused black men and women to begin seeking other means to express their fundamental needs for nurture and self-respect. Since he is unable to find peace, respect, and happiness with the black woman, he considers the white woman to fulfill these needs. The same is true to a lesser extent with black women.

Before the civil rights movement, many black men were attracted to white women. Since most blacks lived in the South before the 1940s, any contact by black men with white women could result in immediate punishment, usually a lynching. Until 1967, there were anti-miscegenation laws (marriages between races) in sixteen states. These laws were overturned by the U.S. Supreme Court.

But during the civil rights movement, large numbers of white women went South to help in the struggle for civil rights. This brought them in contact with black men, and frequently it ended up in sexual liaisons.

Next, the first thing a black man looked for when he came North was a white woman. She had been taboo for him in the South, and he was taught that he was not good enough for her and could not have her. (This does not take into consideration the white woman's desire for black men, sometimes called the *Mandingo* factor.)

However, white men and black women were more acceptable to communities, as it was common for white slave owners to take black mistresses. Even President Jefferson had a black mistress who bore him several children. By the first half of the twentieth century, sexual relations between white men and black women in the South were tolerated if they weren't flaunted.

We know from experience that when a human being is told he cannot have something, it often makes that person want it even more. This was the motivation of many black men migrating to the North. Neither the white woman's appearance nor her character mattered during this time, only her whiteness. She could be ugly, repulsive, unloving, and even disfigured, but during this period, it didn't matter. She was white, and black men were attracted only to that whiteness.

In 1970, there were 65,000 black/white marriages. By 1990, there were 218,000 black/white marriages, 71 percent between black men and white women and 29 percent between black women and white men.

In today's more integrated environment, black men have had an opportunity to compare black women with white women. This comparison goes far deeper than physical features. If any credibility can be attached to many a black woman's caustic comments when she sees a black man with a white woman, comments such as "I don't see what he sees in her," or "She's fat and sloppy," or "I don't understand the brother. He's nice-looking and she looks like nothing," or "If I couldn't do better than that, I wouldn't date a white woman," or "I hope she's got money 'cause her looks are certainly broke," or "It bums me out to see a brother with some unsightly white woman," are often made by black women as passing judgment on black men accompanied by white women.

A segment aired in 1991 on *Prime Time on ABC*, produced by Karen C. Sanders, reported that four times as many black men marry white women as black women marry white men. Why? In Washington, D.C., the black female to black male ratio is estimated at twelve to one, so there's no shortage of eligible black women, yet the black men/white women ratio versus black women/white men ratio holds true there as it does throughout every city and town in America.

According to the *Prime Time* segment, there are twice as many professional black women as there are professional black men in America, nevertheless, professional black men continue to select white women for their spouses. This has caused great friction between the genders because educated black women feel they would have to marry "down" in order to have a family. Many find this unacceptable.

Almost all black clubs, lounges, and bars in larger cities have more women patrons than men. All black churches have at least four times as many black women as black men in their congregation. Since the black woman is so available in all of these places, why is it that there are still so many black men selecting white women?

The availability is there. Certainly, the physical attractiveness is there, since black women spend so much on cosmetics and clothes. Black women are more often better educated and often earn as much or more than the black man. What's not there for the black man? The answer seems simple. What is lacking is peace of mind and a little bit of happiness for the black man, which he finds he can get from the white woman. This peace of mind and happiness stem from the nurturing relationship that he shares with her.

Percy describes such a relationship in the Case of Night and Day.

"I was married for four years to a black woman and it felt like hell. I mean, if it wasn't one thing, it would be something else. She wanted to tell me how to dress, what clothes to buy, when to buy them, and even where to buy them.

"When I got married at twenty-six, I had over nine thousand dollars saved and she went through that in our first year. She had over a hundred pairs of shoes and completely filled our two closets with her clothes. There wasn't any place for me to put my stuff but in the hall closet.

"I'd tell her we were going to set up two separate savings accounts and she agreed, then she would charge so much on plastic that the bill collectors would threaten to take us to court. Three times she spent our rent money, and one time we got evicted from our apartment because we were sixty days overdue.

"She and her girlfriends would lie constantly. I didn't know what to expect next. I don't know how much she cheated on me in those four years, but I'll tell you this. I've got a son with freckles and reddish-brown hair and everybody in my family is blue-black complexioned and all her family members that I've ever met have the same dark complexion.

"I drive a truck interstate, so I'm gone from home three to five days at a time. I'd call home every day and I would think she would be right there when I would call because she would always answer. Well, I found out she arranged for call forwarding to one of her men friend's apartment. My sister found this out. Finally, I just walked away. I quit my job and just stopped payment on everything. I went to court and declared bankruptcy, and after that, I didn't work for a year. After the divorce, she found another man and moved our son in with him. They got married, which was fine with me, because he wasn't my son in the first place.

"After I started driving again, I met this white girl and that's when I stopped going out with any black chicks. You want to know the difference? It's night and day. You get respect from the white woman and disrespect from the black one. You get real care and concern from the white one and you get suckered and used by the black one. You want more, because I can go on all day.

"I mean, my white wife goes out to buy a pair of shoes and she shops around for a good price. They cost one-fourth as much. She's got a lot of clothes, too, but they cost a lot less as she won't buy anything unless I say it's okay. She put all my clothes in one bedroom closet and her clothes in another. She takes care of her clothes and keeps her out-of-season clothes in two cedar chests in the house.

"Sometimes, I have to make her buy things for herself, and she is always trying to buy things for me, plus she works at a full-time job, yet our home is always neat and clean.

"Let me sum it up this way. From my experience, the white woman has learned different values where she shares with you and respects you. She makes you feel like a man. The black woman, all she does is take from you. She may give something here and there, but it's with your own money and she doesn't respect you. She tries to make you feel like a fool."

There are certain words and descriptions that Percy uses that are used by many black men who are married to or date white women: respect, share, trustworthiness, looks up to, makes him feel like a man, care for, concern for. Many of these same men describe black women in totally opposite adjectives: selfish, self-centered, deceptive, bossy, lying, unfaithful, exploitive, noncaring, and punishing.

Many times, the white woman starts out as just a tentative alternative for the black man. He discovers that the sharing, caring, giving, and respect in the relationship are qualities that contribute to his self-esteem.

The black man's haven is a "low-maintenance mate,"

low in financial maintenance and low in emotional maintenance.

With white women, black men learn to develop their capacity to love and care. Black men feel a manliness that they never knew was possible. They are called upon to make the major decisions, and although his spouse may not agree, she will more likely attempt to change his mind through dialogue and discussion.

The problem of racism will always confront the black man and the white woman. This force often strengthens rather than weakens their relationship. The man has decided that the problems associated with marrying or dating a white woman are much less than the amount of discomfort that he experiences from a personal relationship with a typical black woman. Racism is present on the job and in the community, anyway. The relationship with a caring and sharing person offers solace from the daily encounters with racism.

In addition to the racism that most black men encounter when they select a white spouse or girlfriend, there is open hostility from many black women. This attitude is directed at both the white woman and the black man. Often black women will either continuously stare at the white woman accompanying the black man or they will totally ignore her presence when they are talking to the man.

In certain situations, groups of black women have gone so far as to blackball those black men who they discover are dating white women. In Chicago in the sixties and during the seventies, many black public figures such as the late mayor Harold Washington were blackballed by some black women who lived in knowledge-class areas.

These women circulated a list of black men's names with the message "Don't date these men; they date white." Ironically, as these men became more successful, these same black women were falling all over themselves to get attention from these men.

Black men are usually indifferent to black women's attitudes. When they encounter black women's disapproving behavior, they tend to minimize even casual contact with most black women when they are accompanied by their white mates.

Mark has been married twenty-eight years to Joan, who is white and Jewish.

"Joan and I got married and have been the best of friends from the beginning. During the time we got married, I had just finished college and so had Joan. I had worked on steamships as a cook's helper in the summer and even been to Europe a couple of times, so dating white girls wasn't anything new for me. We got married because we loved each other, although we lived together for about a year at first.

"I just got tired of the way black women treated me when I dated them. Nothing was ever simple. I didn't have much money at college. A black date always wanted more than I could afford. So they dropped me. One time my date, a black girl, had me buy three orders of fried shrimp. Can you guess who the third order was for? You got it, her mother. After we ate, I had to rush her home so she could get the shrimp to her mother while it was still hot. I had to starve the next week.

"Anyhow, I stopped seeing black women, especially after I met Joan. Our children are out of college, so we are really free to enjoy traveling now, but it wasn't always that way. After we were married for about six years, I got real depressed and couldn't seem to find myself. I had a brick business, and when the bottom fell out of the market, I went broke. If it hadn't been for Joan, I don't know what I would have done.

"She has a master's in computer sciences and worked steady for seven years while I roamed from one project to the next. I got behind with the IRS and owed them over twenty thousand dollars but she hung right in there with me.

"We make a decision as a family, but it is expected for me to always have the last word and I do. I'm sure there are some white women who don't respect you and don't want you to be the decision maker, but I've never run into them when I was dating.

"People used to stare a lot at Joan and me when we ate out, but that just brought us closer together. Our two children are very light-complexioned and they have Joan's hair and a lot of her features. We always laugh because people would be so confused when they looked at Joan and the two kids and then looked at me with my brown skin and nappy hair. They have her nose and oval-shaped face, but they have my big eyes. We have some beautiful kids.

"Sisters are staring more today than they were back then and they have the nerve to look like they are disgusted at Joan being with me. As far as I'm concerned, that is their personal problem. I can't imagine finding a sister who would have stuck with me when I was down and out those seven years and I wouldn't trade Joan for all the tea in China.

"My son, who is twenty-three, told me recently that he

doesn't think he is going to get involved with any more black girls because of their attitudes. I was almost thirty before I came to that conclusion, so he discovered it much earlier. Sounds to me like everything has gotten worse, but that's not my problem since Joan and I are happy."

Mark and Joan have been married close to thirty years, so their relationship spans the transitional years that reflect the big changes in the black woman's role and the black man's role in marriage and the family. In 1960, it was estimated that 15 percent of the black households were headed by a female as compared with 58 percent today. Mark mentioned that he experienced the beginning of what is very prevalent today regarding the black woman's behavior toward the black man. It is this very same behavior that encourages many young men to seek out the low-maintenance woman who may or may not be white but is seldom black.

Black GIs, as a result of the U.S. involvement in wars overseas, have met and married Vietnamese and Korean women. Typically, Asian women believe that respect and control are part of man's nature and grow up subservient to the male, so they tend to show their respect in every way possible. This is also true of Japanese women. It is not unusual for an Asian woman to give her husband a rubdown every night, fix his food, and do anything for her man. Black women are astonished that women with such behavior exist.

The culture and families in which these women grew up have a great deal to do with their attitudes about men. They believe that the man is in control at all times. Although there are some exceptions to this rule, it is rare. They are very frugal in their spending habits and don't ask for or require a lot of money in a relationship with the man. The traits found in these Asian women bring the black man satisfaction and respect and often a worry-free environment.

Another group of women who do not require or ask for as much from the black man is the older black woman who dates a younger black man. Although she will use the arsenal at the slightest opportunity to manipulate, such manipulation is far more infrequent since she expects less of him than she did in her youth. Her needs tend to be more personal, like companionship, frequent sex, and mothering, rather than cash and expensive gifts. In fact, she will often absorb more of their expenses now that she has usually accumulated much more than he has. It's a turnabout.

In this kind of relationship, often there are certain understandings on either person's part. He can be exploitive and immature, seeking to be cared for and yet not caring in return. He serves her sexual and social needs, while in return she serves his dependency needs. But the turnabout in reality is the same old thing: "You look after my needs and I look after yours." Even if there is great regard between the parties, these relationships don't often last.

Jerry describes his experience with an older woman after his divorce. He says she was a safe refuge for him.

"I stayed with Ivory six months after I divorced my wife. I was so tired of the pressure from Candy, my ex-wife, that when Ivory showed she was interested in me, I just said the hell with age. Ivory at fifty-one was attractive with a sparkling personality. I was twenty-six, but we got along well. We talked a lot and would often go to cocktail parties. She was a chemistry professor at a Big Ten university and I taught high school biology, so we had many interests in common.

"At first, it was just peaceful not to be nagged at and asked for things all the time. Ivory bought me a word processor when she found out I wanted one. Then she bought me a used car, but that's when I started feeling uneasy about our relationship. She had been married and divorced three times, all to professional men. While I knew she could afford these presents, I felt uneasy. I started feeling like a kept man, which I wasn't, as I shared costs with her.

"When we went out, people would look at me like I was her young stud, and when I had some friends over to her house, she would ask me to make them leave by ten o'clock during the week. Sometimes she would stroll through the living room from the kitchen and remind me in front of my guests that it was getting close to ten. This was especially the case if the guests were female associates from school.

"She always wanted to make sure that when she went to sleep, I was in the bed with her. After a while, I felt like a child rather than a grown man. It began to eat away at me. One day when she was teaching class, I drove the car she bought me to the campus and parked right beside her car. I left a typed note on her windshield thanking her for everything and telling her that it was time for me to pick up the pieces of my life and move on.

"In the car were the word processor and a dozen white roses, which were her favorite. Then I caught a plane to New York and have never seen her again.

"I really liked Ivory, but I could never love her. She was too set in her ways and she was beginning to flaunt things in my face. She didn't show me the respect I expected. It wasn't what I wanted in my life."

Jerry is honest about his relationship with Ivory. Sharing expenses created financial benefits. He also obtained stability from the relationship. He was also aware of why he was involved with Ivory and the need to terminate the relationship while giving back the expensive gifts he received from her. Though he is not the typical young stud who exploits a relationship with an older woman for money and gifts, he is typical in his need to find a haven.

Another type of woman that some well-educated black men seek as a haven is one he could never accept as a mate and whose value system and class level are different from his. He will probably relate to two of these women at the same time. He may even budget how much money and time he will spend each month on them. And if one requests more attention or financial assistance than he budgeted, he will drop her and find a replacement, expressing very little sadness in the parting. This same type of black man may select a black female considerably younger than he is. In this type of situation, he usually attempts to mold her into the type of woman he can bring up to his standards. This usually fails.

Most of these black men are professionals from the knowledge class. The women they date are typical black women, and these men have protected their Achilles' heels with cold, realistic attitudes about the women— attitudes that prevent them from truly caring. The probability is that he wouldn't know a decent woman if he fell over her. This is demonstrated in the Case of No Ladies Allowed.

Bob is a genuine bachelor. At forty-three, he has been

engaged four times, yet he has never married or had children. Self-employed as a consultant, his annual income is approximately $60,000.

"I prefer to date young, attractive women from the far side of town and try to train them to be something better than what they are. When I say younger, I mean early twenties. I feel like Pygmalion as I try to make them over. I enjoy their company, their energy, their vivaciousness. I know they're in it to get what they can, while I enjoy teaching them and exposing them to a better life. As long as they stay within my budget, we get along fine.

"Although I am sometimes surprised, I don't expect too much out of them because they usually have few positive values and little to offer intellectually. I select them primarily because I know I could never marry one of them.

"I don't make any commitments and I recognize that they aren't capable of sincere love. They all have whorish ways, which is fine with me. Naturally, there are some corporate affairs that I won't take them to. For those, I have a couple of good friends to use as partners.

"Though they respect me, I don't really respect them. I'm blunt. I tell them they don't qualify for my kind of life, but if they want to stick around, I'll help them, teach them manners, improve their language, take them places, advise them, and teach them to pass as 'quality' women. Most of the time, I end up dropping them. Once in a while a smart one would drop me. One read me the riot act and say, 'You're using me like a tampon and throwing me into the toilet. You're using me—it's not the other way around.'

"Then I just look for a replacement. I have only one principle with black women. No ladies allowed. With a lady, you fall in love, plan a family, and share a life. She respects you and you respect her. Where do you find such a woman? I am better off with one who isn't a lady in the first place.

"When I run into one who is a lady, I back off because I don't want to get emotionally involved."

This tells us more about Bob than he realizes. He may be smart, he may do well financially, but he is shallow, selfish, and smug. To a black woman on his own level who is smart and perceptive, it would be apparent quickly. Probably the women he admires most are the ones who see through him and reject him. So the members of the No Ladies Allowed Club—other black men like Bob—also don't really feel comfortable dating white women and don't understand intelligent black women. The end result is that they date low-maintenance women (another term for lower-class women they can use cheaply).

Consequently, these men will have multiple relationships, adding or dropping a woman as time and money allow. Each relationship seldom lasts more than six months.

Some wealthy black men in the knowledge class use money to "buy" a relationship (once known as a "kept woman"). They even live by the Golden Rule. That is, he who has the gold makes the rule. This type of relationship is based on a mutual understanding. He is either divorced, single, or separated from his wife.

He does it for his reasons and she does it for hers. The woman understands that he might terminate the relationship at the slightest provocation and he understands that she will leave him if she ever falls in love or attracts a more generous power broker. The relationship is strictly one of convenience and love has little if anything to do with it.

This is quite similar to certain white actors in Hollywood who have strange problems. They are the ones who are afraid every woman is after his money (which may or may not be true); he may be a homosexual and is obliged to hide it with a "relationship" (like Rock Hudson and others); he may be bisexual, which would leave him open to blackmail and AIDS.

The black man in this group uses the relationship either as a "cover" or to shelter himself from becoming emotionally involved with a black woman who might make him unhappy and share his wealth and/or peace of mind.

Since the power broker makes no emotional investment, he does not reap any, either. He may pay for the black woman's apartment, its upkeep, and her clothes. She will be on a "salary" and she has to be available when he so desires. If he's straight, sex may be involved. If he's kinky, she is no doubt agreeable to his abnormal tastes. If he's homosexual, she simply has to be seen with him and put on an act. Any sexual relations she has must be kept under wraps. Some of these black women are elegant-looking, usually light-skinned, with great figures, who may be out-of-work actresses. It serves their purpose to keep up a front they normally can't afford.

This black man tends to live a somewhat isolated and lonely life while in his haven. An extreme example of this is the Case of They Call Me Mr. Malone.

Mike Malone is a successful criminal attorney whose thriving practice nets him an income of over $400,000 annually, according to Donna, his girlfriend of the past three years.

"When we are out, I address him as Mr. Malone or Attorney Malone because he wants it that way. I drink heavily sometimes and he doesn't like it when I slip and call him Mike in front of some of his friends. I get yelled at as soon as we are alone.

"He is nice to me, but I'm never allowed to question anything he does and often he refuses to introduce me to his associates. We will be dining out and someone will come up to our table and start talking. They might gab for ten minutes and he'll finish the conversation without introducing me. I think that is most impolite, but that is the way he is and I accept it. It used to bother me, but it doesn't anymore.

"Now and then I quietly date some men who I think are better than Mike, but they can't keep me in the style he can and they are not as much fun. He's good to me, but we don't love each other."

Some of the black men who fit into this group use the black woman as their haven by playing the role of the other man, as opposed to being a spare man or a main man. It's a matter of ego. He is not exactly her main man, as he sees her only at his convenience, letting her be on his arm at parties, conventions, and conferences. He may require her to meet him at some out-of-town destination or for only a one-night rendezvous. Any sex is at his request only.

He commands the respect of his peers and is not interested in the terms "main man" or "spare man." But he ignores her as a woman and is not entangled with her as a whole person because of the emotional distance that he maintains. To him, she is simply another expense-account item, nothing more. To her, it's as though she were acting another role on stage.

If he is married, she may serve as an occasional relief from his wife, but she is neither his mistress nor concubine. She is his recreation, his plaything. In other words, he has taken on the trapping of a decadent, wealthy white man. When he feels any hassle or discomfort with this arrangement, he terminates it.

The only black woman who offers a permanent refuge for the black man is the *right* black woman. She has high standards and positive values, which she will not alter for material gain. She respects the individual black man who meets her standards and is willing to share and risk her feelings with her man. Although she may be very assertive, or even aggressive, she understands the black man's sensitivity to the stereotype and accepts his need for dominance in a relationship and thus expects him to make final decisions. She does not believe in nor does she practice the spare man and main man roles. She is straightforward, and whatever she tells her spouse or man will be the truth. Secure in herself, she has a healthy, strong self-esteem and is not self-centered or selfish. She understands the current fragility of the black man/black woman relationship, so she understands the importance of the man's being in control and tries to strengthen his weaknesses. There is no desire to change him.

She doesn't accept financial assistance for her everyday needs and wants and is supportive in whatever he is involved in. Her confidence level and expectations of him are very high and infidelity on her part is out of the question, regardless of the circumstances. Usually independent to the extent that she relies solely on her own integrity to handle her part of the relationship, she expects the same from him, so it fills all of her needs and some of her wants.

She has few girlfriends, but those she does have are generally self-supporting and have similar positive standards upon which to base their lives. She reflects none of the Sapphire characteristics and usually is a product of a very strong male parent–dominated family. After marriage, she contributes to her spouse's success with moral support. She believes in the work ethic and will continue working.

Is she the perfect black woman? Perhaps not, because we were taught to believe that you find perfection only in Heaven. But she is certainly the ideal black woman. She is neither above him nor below him, but considers him her equal.

She refuses to use black men and equally refuses to be used by black men. She has a clear image of her black man and recognizes his weaknesses and his strengths. She refuses to compromise her standards when selecting friends. She has a companion relationship with her mate and clearly perceives their respective roles. Said one black woman psychologist at a focus group, "The right couple are husband and wife, lovers and best friends. This is the basis for a wonderful relationship."

Since she presents such an exceptional profile compared with many black women, a black man with similar values and standards will immediately find peace of mind and happiness in their relationship. Instead of conflict, there is compatibility, both enjoying a haven that consists of a harmonious relationship. The Case of Friends, Then Lovers reflects such a bond.

Mahogany and Tracy are both twenty-seven-year-old women who are seriously involved with their boyfriends. Each one describes the expectations in her present relationship.

"I have certain things that I expect when I meet any man that I am going to date," Tracy says. "First, they have to be saved because religion is very important to me, and, second, he has to have some goals in life. Third, he has to have a life of his own and let me have a life of my own.

"Since my father died last year, I have taken over his accounting business and it has grown. I've just finished passing my CPA exams, so now I can devote full-time to expanding the company. The man I choose to spend my life with has to be strong enough to let me grow and at the same time be able to control me in a sensible way.

"Like right now, he makes me quit work on Fridays at 5:00 P.M., when I used to work until 10:00 P.M. and come right back to the office on Saturday morning. He says I have to relax and take the weekend off so we can enjoy ourselves and each other.

"While I don't expect and don't want him giving me clothes or money, other than flowers or maybe perfume for my birthday, I do expect him to take me to nice places to eat or movies or dancing. He doesn't have to buy me personal items, after all, I'm self-supporting—that's what I make money for. But I do like to do interesting things. Sometimes, it doesn't cost anything as long as we do it together. If it costs a lot, I always offer to go Dutch treat. Last weekend, we went to the zoo and had lunch and it cost less than twenty dollars. Yesterday, we went to see a play at the Regal Theater and the tickets cost eighty dollars. So, you see, it is not the spending a lot of money that is important to me. It's being able to do what we want to do together.

"I think you have to like each other and be friends first, before you can fall in love. I'm almost afraid to brag about our relationship because I haven't ever been serious with anyone before. I felt that if I couldn't find a man who had my values, I'd refuse to lower my standards and compromise my ideals.

"Mahogany and I are first cousins and we kind of grew up together. We discuss our career goals all the time, but rarely discuss our social lives."

Mahogany interrupts, pointing out, "Though Tracy is pretty, she worked hard and never had much of a social life for the past five years while I was socially active. I'd go crazy if I had to do what Tracy did. I dated a lot, but most of the black men that I came in contact with were losers. They were all bad news. I don't go to church that much, and they certainly don't have to be saved, but they should have some purpose in life, some goals. I don't want him to buy me anything. I can buy whatever it is that I want. I want him to be able to plan and make decisions and not try to live off of me.

"I work as a consultant for a federal agency now, but someday I want my own business like Tracy. I'll have a life and I want my husband to have a life, too. Right now, the guy that I go with lives a thousand miles away from here. We talk once or twice a week on the phone and see each other once or twice a month. We are very secure with each other. I trust he is doing the right thing and he trusts that I am, too. I don't worry about our relationship as I know we both think alike."

Said Tracy, "Well, I'm keeping my fingers crossed with my boyfriend. We've been seeing each other now for six months and we know we believe in the same things. Each day I say, so far, so good. I've been looking for the right man for five years and if it doesn't work out, I just won't have anybody to go out with for a while."

"I'm different," Mahogany says. "If I didn't have Ralph, I'd date somebody to socialize. I would go nuts doing it like Tracy. That doesn't mean I'd find the right man any faster than she did. There are many black men out there with absolutely nothing on their mind but three things, sex, sex, and sex. Now I love to make love, but there is a time and place for everything and sex is not the thing to do until you are positive about the man you are dating."

"Yes," Tracy agrees. "I want a man with character who knows there is a time and place for everything. If we don't have common values, I won't want to have sex or spend a lot of time with him."

"Look, I want to eventually marry a man I can respect and look up to," Mahogany says. "That is an important part of happiness."

Young women like Tracy and Mahogany have the right outlook to build a stable family. A stable family and home is every man's ideal haven. It is the only goal that will insure the survival of the black man and his community.

CHAPTER

10

The Black Man's Survival Kit

On January 7, 1994, prominent black leaders and politicians held a conference in Washington, D.C., to discuss the runaway statistics involving young black men in America. They all agreed that black crime is spinning out of control.

Though there was agreement something had to be done, few answers were available as to why the number of black criminals in prison had tripled since the 1980s. Congress was certain to pass a bill to spend over $20 billion during the next five years to increase police forces around the country by 100,000 and build more prisons.

Most of the leaders, including members of the Black Caucus (black congressmen and congresswomen), would prefer that the bill place emphasis on education and crime prevention. It was pointed out that crimes by blacks against blacks have quadrupled in the past few years, particularly in black neighborhoods. C. Dolores Tucker, head of the National Political Congress of Black Women, lashed out at rap music that calls for violence against black women.

In the end, the general agreement seemed to be that the solutions would be extremely difficult, extremely costly, and had to be long-term. It's like the weather. As Mark Twain is reported to have said, "Everybody talks about the weather but nobody does anything about it." Perhaps nothing can be done about the weather, but something must be done to restore black society. It can be done only by restoring the black family in America, and it can be done, not by more police and prisons, but only by blacks themselves.

Congressman Kweisi Mfume of Maryland, one of the leaders of the Black Caucus, who attended the January conference of black leaders, said again, in an interview on *Meet the Press*, the $20 billion to be spent on prisons would be better spent on crime prevention. As for more prisons, he suggested using the closed army bases to incarcerate criminals.

The Long Road Ahead

The Chinese proverb says, "A journey of a thousand miles begins with a single step." The first step for any solution for saving the African-American male must be based on the assumption that there are enough black men who are mature, responsible, and determined to overcome the crisis facing black America.

W. E. B. Du Bois always stressed that "the black race of

America can survive and prosper if ten percent lead and do the proper thing."

This talented 10 percent, the leaders, must be made up of black men who already have their own lives under control. They must adhere to a prescribed set of rules that will be called the Black Man's Survival Kit. It is intended to insure the survival of the black man, which in turn insures the survival of the black family.

The List

This kit begins with a unique list of questions about a standard of conduct written in 1896, almost one hundred years ago. It was published by the Premier Publishing Company in a book entitled *The College of Life*. This seven-hundred-page book was written to instruct American blacks on how to act and conduct themselves after slavery had been abolished. Under "The Guide to Success," it stated: "A good man not only forbears those gratifications which are forbidden by reason and religion, but even restrains himself in unforbidden instances."

This advice is still relevant today and should act as a guide for the talented one-in-ten black men, those leaders who will restore black families and reunite black communities that are tearing themselves apart. The survival kit's list of questions will heighten the black man's self-awareness about his forbearance and restraint. Here are the questions:

1. Am I mentally and spiritually strong enough?
2. Am I a mature adult?

3. Am I able to control my life and refuse to compromise on those matters that produce strong black families?
4. Am I willing to set an example for other black males to prove what genuine black manhood is?
5. Am I willing to challenge those black men and women whose actions tear apart the black family?
6. Do I believe that black men and black women, as equal partners, can restore the black family?
7. Can I support the goal that the black man in the black family should once again be head of the household?
8. Am I willing to maintain my self-esteem with positive attitudes?
9. Am I willing to request the respect of black women because of my values, as I respect her for hers?
10. Will I use all means possible to raise the responsibility consciousness of black men and women?

This list is not complete, but should be expanded by each individual based on his own circumstances. To insure survival of the black community, honesty will be the foundation upon which each individual must build. The black man who answers yes to these questions is ready to move to the next item of the survival kit.

The Mirror

The next item in the kit is a mirror. Each one-in-ten leader must face a mirror and take a long, hard look at himself. What kind of male does he see? Does the reflec-

tion show a person in touch with himself who understands the meaning of black public responsibility?

What he does in private is his personal right. What he
does in public, in the workplace, on the street, and how
he relates to others, both black and white, is a responsibility he cannot ignore.

There is a line between personal freedom and personal
responsibility. If a black male produces a baby, it is his
private affair. But it becomes a public affair if the baby he
produces becomes a cocaine addict, gang banger, drug
dealer, killer, or a welfare recipient. The black man must
handle his responsibilities regardless of his class.

Still facing the mirror, if the black male sees the reflec-
tion of a man who is on welfare, or a man who has
abandoned his children, or a man who is promiscuous, he
is seeing a liability to society and to himself. The man who
reflects such a liability is a threat to black survival. He,
himself, will not survive. He must be willing to accept
change. He must be able to answer yes to all questions
posed on the list.

The Motto

The third item in the kit is a sign that says, "Do the right
thing!" This motto dictates how the black male should
relate to the black woman. This sign should be posted in a
place where the black man can see it constantly; on the
bathroom mirror, on the back of the clothes closet door,
and over the bed.

Doing the right thing means respecting the black
woman and, by example, becoming a role model for all

black youths. Doing the right thing means no use of violence. It means walking away from the promiscuous behavior that is a direct route to AIDS. It means resisting
sexual enticement. It means placing a value on your life.
It means connecting with a woman on wholesome terms.

The Case of Nothing But a Man is an example of how to
do the right thing:

Scott's father was a physician in Atlanta, as was his
grandfather. Scott chose to become a businessman instead and obtained his education from the University of
Chicago, where he received an M.B.A. as well as a Ph.D.
in psychology. When he returned to Atlanta, Scott set up
one of the first HMOs (health maintenance organizations) in the state and, with his father and grandfather,
invested heavily in the stock market. At thirty-six, Scott
was still a bachelor with no children. He was a member of
several boards of nonprofit organizations, traveled
monthly to Washington, D.C., as a consultant to a federal
agency, and lectured at Morehouse College.

Although he had a work schedule that required sixty to
seventy hours a week, Scott made time for female relationships that were mature and mutually fulfilling. Scott
relates a recent incident that a weaker, immature man
would have handled differently.

"I've had occasions to have women out to my house
many times just for drinks or recreation. We play tennis or
swim and even skinny-dip sometimes. But if they come off
with a 'I've got what you want' or 'I've got what you need'
attitude, I am very quick to reject them," he explains. "Last
month I made a bad choice. I invited two friendly women,
both cute and very personable, over to my place. One was
a beautician and the other a social worker.

"Well," he continued, "while the three of us were sitting by the pool, the beautician, whom I'll call Lavelle, excused herself to go to the bathroom. I told her where it was and continued to talk with her friend. As soon as she left, her friend immediately began to flirt with me. I ignored her advances and continued to make small talk.

"A few minutes later, Lavelle's voice blares out over my intercom system asking me if I would please come upstairs. She needed something and couldn't find it. So I left her friend at the pool and went into the bathroom off my living room, but she was not there. When I pressed the intercom and asked Lavelle where she was, she said upstairs in the bathroom. I still didn't catch on to what was going on until I walked into my master bedroom, which is connected to the upstairs bathroom, and there she was, lying naked on top of my bed.

"I was shocked at first. There was no way that I could have been prepared for that," he explained. "She told me that she had wanted me all evening and just couldn't wait any longer. I tried to be polite by telling her that it wouldn't be right to do this with her friend waiting downstairs by herself, but she made it clear that her friend wouldn't mind being alone. Actually, she would be willing to join in. Then she showed me part of her anatomy, which I prefer not to discuss. I asked her to get dressed and she refused. So I just walked out and left her upstairs naked.

"After about thirty minutes, she rejoined us downstairs and both women left shortly after that. They never got another invitation to my home.

"Oh, I should tell you," he added, "a few weeks later, when I was talking to a friend of mine at the Rotary

Club, he told me that his wife had been to Lavelle's beauty salon and that she was informing everyone how immaculate my house was, but how she personally wouldn't want to have anything to do with me because I was gay." Scott smiled. "Her problem was that she ran into a man who was nothing but a man and she couldn't deal with it."

It is interesting that Scott did not discuss any sexual aspects of this experience or even make derogatory remarks about the two women. He was in control the entire time. Even when he related that the beautician was slandering his reputation in her salon, Scott focused on his manhood rather than trying to prove he had rejected her or that the accusations were false.

He showed that he has too much respect for himself and would not stoop to Lavelle's level by making derogatory remarks about her. Scott projects a very strong sense of self-esteem and self-respect.

Although "Do the right thing" means being strong when encountering a seductive woman like Lavelle, it also means supporting, sharing, and encouraging the black woman who expects a mature, wholesome relationship. It means complimenting her on her strengths and sharing responsibility with her. Whether she is young, middle-aged, or older should not matter when it comes to the black man's giving support to this type of woman at all times. Conversely, it means giving no support or attention to Sapphires and aspiring Sapphires.

"Do the right thing" sends a loud and clear message to the Sapphires. Women who are too selfish to receive this message are guaranteed ostracism from the mainstream from a wholesome black America.

The Cards

The next item in the survival kit is a package of three-by-five index cards. When a man is seriously considering a long-term involvement with a woman, cards become the basis for survival used to measure the worth of a relationship. (A woman may use this assessment when considering a husband.)

The man writes one of the woman's undesirable characteristics on a single card. He uses as many cards as she has undesirable characteristics. These traits should include behavioral aspects of her character. For instance, if she tells the man she loves him, but her actions indicate that she doesn't, then one of the cards would have on it the word "lies." So the negative items on the cards may read:

1. Lies.
2. Boasts of her affairs.
3. Self-centered.
4. Insists always on having her way.
5. Nags or whines.
6. Indolent and sloppy.
7. Deceitful.
8. Requests money for favors.
9. Steals.
10. Contradicts constantly.

The cards that have the undesirable traits comprise the *negative suit*.

He then uses cards to make a *positive suit*. Some of the

characteristics that could be written on the cards in the positive suit:

1. Intelligent.
2. Well-educated.
3. Religious.
4. Neat and clean.
5. Honest and dependable.
6. Admits mistakes.
7. Sense of humor.
8. Likes children.
9. Has a good reputation.
10. Considerate.

A characteristic should be the result of each black man's preferences. What annoys one black may not be an irritant to another. However, no black man likes to share his woman with another man, so the spare man appears as a negative. The same is true about stubbornness. So "stubborn" would be listed on a negative card.

Assign a number from one to ten to each characteristic on each card. Ten will be the highest number given to the most aggravating characteristics in the negative suit and the highest number for the most attractive characteristics in the positive suit. It will soon be apparent whether the woman should be part of a man's life.

If she is not to be part of his life, he should keep the cards in the negative suit handy and memorize them. Every time she comes to mind, he should take out the negative cards and look at them. When she calls him on the phone, he should look at the cards while talking with her. If she was his wife and he meets his "ex" at a gathering or while shopping, he should review the cards in his mind.

If he begins to think of her positive attributes (if any), he must remember they did not overcome the negative aspects. He should condition himself to seeing the negative cards with her face on them.

Sometimes, the dark side of a person has a strong magnetic attraction for a man or a woman. This negative association bailout must then be practiced over and over again. When he goes to sleep, if his thoughts turn to her, he should review the negative characteristics like counting sheep. At no time should he be without his cards until he is completely turned off by the thought of her. He should make extra sets and keep them readily available in the places where he is most often.

There is more to marriage than sex. If the man starts thinking about her sexually, he should concentrate even more on the negative cards. Of course, there are times when a man decides he wants the woman despite her negative connotations. When that happens (like in *Porgy and Bess*), then there is little one can do to combat it.

However, for the most part, the negative association game will work. Every time the negative feelings are triggered, they create a turnoff. These negative reactions become mentally glued to the woman with whom they are associated. Slowly but surely the thought of the woman herself becomes a turnoff.

On the other side of the coin, a woman should make up her set of negative and positive cards as a litmus test for the man she is interested in.

The man or woman discovers that when any emotions of sorrow or sense of loss that the termination caused are gone, he/she has been emotionally healed.

The Help Book

For the man, an essential item in the survival kit is a small notebook with the names and phone numbers of friends who can provide a support group. This notebook is the *help* book. The number of men listed in the help book should probably be no more than five or six. They will be responsible men who are usually close acquaintances or family.

Men in general, and black men in particular, have difficulty talking to other men about their problems with women. They don't want to admit they are suffering distress caused by the breakup. They believe that such emotion is unmanly. These men should realize that many black men experience the same problems and that they can find comfort within a support group. By talking with the men in his support group, the man in distress will find out how others view his situation. They can relate how they handled their own breakups. Talks with support group members are therapeutic and may only be as infrequent as weekly conversations. Meetings over dinner or for coffee or drinks are more preferable encounters. These discussions will strengthen the man's resolve, relieve the pain, and more importantly help him think clearly about his future relationships with women.

Often it is the small advice that can make a major difference. As one friend confided to another, "Don't go to a bar or lounge alone when you feel depressed, because that is when you're the most vulnerable. Don't begin a new relationship," he advised. Black men who themselves are not involved in a destructive relationship are going to be of great comfort and counsel to the man who has left such circumstances.

That's the situation that happened to Guy. Three of his old friends got together with him at home and each gave him his candid opinions about the relationship from which he just escaped. Two of them were married, one was single; two were his age and one much older. All three men had the same goal: to help Guy get through his crisis. Though their views of the woman in question varied, their view of the relationship was consistent.

They were determined to assist Guy to exorcise the past and help find more suitable female friends. As the older black man suggested, "It can happen to any of us. We must help each other by discussing painful truths. We have to help our brother understand that he did the right thing by ending the relationship. We make him realize that he has to get on with his life. That's what the black man's survival is all about."

One More Item

The survival kit contains one more item—a package of condoms. Responsible black men are too valuable an asset to the future of the black community to practice unsafe sex. Sex can be beautiful and deadly. While it is a necessary ingredient in an enduring relationship, the act should not put the parties at risk. As discussed earlier in this book, black communities (men, women, and their offspring) are experiencing a high increase in the incidence of AIDS and other sexually transmitted diseases. Proper care and precaution must be taken.

Summary

Nothing in the survival kit is expensive. All the items are readily available to anyone. The black man who employs the items in the kit with the techniques explained will be a leader in the one-in-ten group, as it proves he has taken control of his life. He will survive.

He will survive to lead, to teach, and to help build a strong black America, as well as a stronger America dedicated to freedom and opportunity for all its citizens.

The Right to Know

The purpose of the Black Man's Survival Kit is to help him take those actions necessary to insure a viable future. The techniques used will help him understand himself and the challenges he faces as he grows to responsible manhood. He must become self-aware, have pride in his black heritage, and have self-esteem. He must first set his own life in order. Then, with the positive knowledge of who he is, he can set out to help his community.

A self-aware person is one with the confidence to insist on honest and open relationships with others. The black man who has achieved self-confidence has earned the right to know the truth about the woman with whom he may begin a relationship.

And the truth will prevent him from having experiences such as these:

"When we got married, I didn't know that she was

HIV positive," said Jim, an accountant and college grad-
uate.

"I inherited bills for nineteen thousand dollars on her
credit cards. I wish I had known about it before we got
married," Sidney said.

Hakeem said, "Three of her aunts told me she was a
tramp—right in our own kitchen. It was depressing. All I
could say was, 'I wish I had known before we jumped that
broom and got married.' "

"I hadn't a clue she was on crack before the baby was
born. I wasn't suspicious for a moment because she never
drank or took drugs when we dated," Clarence said. "She
was shy and acted like the most innocent, baby-faced girl
I'd ever met. When it all came to light, I told her I'd stick
with her if she agreed to go into rehab. She agreed, then
she tried to kill herself. She was placed in a mental hospital for observation. The doctor showed me her record.
This was her third suicide attempt.

"After we got married the insurance company dropped
me when I tried to add her to my health insurance policy.
She had HIV positive and it was not in remission. She put
my life in jeopardy, yet she never told me."

The Four Rs

Today, black men should avoid the surprises described
above by practicing the four Rs: research, research, research, and research. Hell, wealthy people, both black
and white, do it. Should parents allow their son or daughter to marry anyone without due diligence?

It's important for everyone to investigate a prospective

mate in this age of anxiety. He should research the woman's background, her friends, her health, and her finances. This could be done through private investigation agencies.

Her Background

A black woman's family should be the first area covered in a background check. The prospective groom should try to meet all the members of the household in which she grew up. The apple never falls far from the tree. He should carefully check out Mama and Grandmama, especially when there is not a dominant man in the immediate family. Is her mother and/or grandmother the type of woman that he would want as a lifetime companion years later? Would he be content or satisfied living with someone like her mother?

If she proves to be a woman of character, it makes no difference whether she is rich or poor. If he is to survive his relationship with his choice of a black woman, he must look closely at her mother's relationships and interactions and how she maintains her household. In most cases, the mother is the model and the daughter will manage relationships in the same way. He should examine closely how her mother supports herself and the family, how the mother perceives and relates to men, and how truthful and honest she is with others.

If her mother has never been a wife, can he expect his fiancée to know how a wife relates to her husband? He should note how the mother feels about men in general, and if she is advising her daughter about him. If he identifies disrespect or dishonesty in the mother, he should evaluate if these attitudes exist in the daughter.

Michael did not pay attention to the behavior of his future mother-in-law while he was dating Jean. He knew her mother was a nurse who worked in a hospital. She would frequently obtain for him prescription medication for his ulcers. This saved him almost $200 a month. She refused payment for the medication.

It never dawned on Michael that she might be stealing from the hospital. One day, Michael discovered that his Rolex watch and a diamond ring were missing from his apartment after Jean had been there. "I called the police," he said, "and I pressed charges. Jean got away with it because her mother swore that she had been home with her all day. This must have been planned, as they knew I'd find out. The mother was a liar and both turned out to be thieves. I'm out a few thousand bucks, but I'm lucky because I was going to ask her to marry me," Michael admitted.

Family gatherings, house parties, church socials, and club parties provide opportunities to observe family members. The alert black man can determine the extent of honesty, respect, self-esteem, and caring among family members. If persons in the family score poorly in these areas, in all probability, so will she. He should be skeptical if she behaves one way with her family and differently with him.

The absence of a male in the family will be enlightening. If there aren't any men in the immediate family such as a father or grandfather, the aware man will be cautious. The women in the family will not be used to relating to an independent, strong black man. The man should examine closely the causes for the absence of males in the immediate family *before* deciding to continue the relationship. The aware black man realizes that he can't change lifelong attitudes. If he doesn't have the respect of the woman and the other females in the family, he should move on.

If there are men in the immediate family, he should get to know them and determine what role they play as decision makers, disciplinarians, and providers. Is a man the head of the household or in the way of a household? Our aware man must answer this question, since he very likely will find himself in the same position if he shares a home with a woman from this background.

It is also easy to learn about a woman's background from sources outside her immediate family. The aware man will usually know some of the people who live in her neighborhood or community. If the woman has returned to the community after attending school or starting a career, the use of a private investigator in her previous location is a good idea. The cost of a few days of this service is not very much to insure that a relationship remains honest, open, and healthy. (If she is smart and sincere, she will be doing the same thing.)

If a man wants the relationship to grow and last, he has the right to get answers about the woman. Whom has she dated? Has she been known to use drugs or alcohol? What kind of person was she in school? On the job? Can she be trusted? He should pursue the answers to these questions tactfully but aggressively. The stakes are too great not to use as many sources as possible to get this information.

Her Girlfriends

The second area he should research very carefully involves her girlfriends. There is a lot of truth in the old adage "Birds of a feather flock together." These women won't be as much on their guard when they are around him (unless they're jealous). Often, they do the same things his woman does or says.

Duke found this out. He believed that his fiancée's girlfriends were different from her. He thought the ideas and attitudes they expressed were very different from those of his future wife. On several occasions before he was married, he listened as several of her girlfriends talked negatively about Johnny Carson for not being more generous with his ex-wives (who reportedly received millions in settlements). They insisted that a wife should grab all she could. His woman disagreed. She often told him in private how wrong her girlfriends were for saying that. So they got married. But can you guess the first thing she did when she left? She took all the money out of their joint bank account and charged all their credit cards to the max, then turned around and said, "I don't intend to leave you with anything to give to another woman."

Duke shook his head from side to side and said, "I should have paid attention to the way her girlfriends carried on. They were really speaking her mind."

The aware man will watch the buying, shopping, and leisure habits of her girlfriends. Do they compete with each other in terms of dress, lifestyles, men, and possessions? Most of the time, if the black man listens carefully, the girlfriends will give clues about their activities and talk about how they hoodwinked boyfriends, their latest acquisitions, and how they conceal things from their men.

The aware man will notice if they treat each other with respect. What kind of relationships do they have with men? What do their men say when they double- or triple-date? If they have children, how do they treat them? The object of the man's affection is going to relate to others in the same way her close girlfriends do. If her friends' behavior is characterized by Sapphire traits, he should bail out pronto. If he chooses to ignore these warning signs, he has only himself to blame when the relationship turns sour.

Her Health

If a man and a woman want to build a life together, that means that they must give up their privacy. One of the conditions of relinquishing privacy is revealing the overall state of one's physical health. It is your body, but a commitment to a relationship means that your body is now the other's as well. Your individual lives, in other words, are now each other's.

The aware man should go through a complete physical examination and so should the woman. Each has the right to review the results. Both physicals should include the test for the HIV virus. If there are medical liabilities or fertility problems, both parties must be aware of the extent of these conditions. The man who attempts to build a lasting relationship under any other circumstances is a fool.

Her Finances

It is not uncommon for young people to have incurred some financial debt, particularly if they borrowed money to pay for their college education or training. The repayment schedules for education loans can be met if the person has a steady job. The same is true of repayment schedules for car loans. The aware man won't be surprised if a woman has these financial commitments.

The surprises he must avoid are the debts that are the result of indiscriminate spending, a common Sapphire trait. An aware man will ask for documentation of the woman's financial condition, like all (not just some) credit cards and bank statements. The man should not be embarrassed to make such a request; likewise, he should make his records available to her.

If the woman has moved several times during the last two years, it may be an indication that she doesn't pay her rent. Or she can't live within a realistic budget. Or the addresses belong to former male friends.

If, during the review of her finances, the man discovers that another man has co-signed a loan for a big-ticket item like a car, he should determine exactly what her relationship is with that man. He must also demand a straightforward answer to this question: "How come he was willing to co-sign this loan?"

Obviously, her answer will have a significant effect on the future (or no future) of the relationship.

No Compromise

If the aware man is so attracted to a woman with whom he is thinking about a lifetime relationship, he has to employ the four Rs. He must make no compromise to this approach. He should proceed tactfully and with respect for the woman's feelings and sense of privacy, but he must be diligent and thorough. And she should have the opportunity to investigate him.

There are people who will object to the four-Rs approach. They think it is too objective and "cold-blooded." They argue that it destroys romance and implies a lack of trust. People who feel this way don't (or won't) understand the present nature of relations between black men and black women. The naïve blacks who argue for romance and trust will learn soon enough that water is wet, all fires are hot, and all intimate relationships (black or white) require vigilance.

Some notions of romance are based entirely upon the moment. These notions have nothing to do with survival and tomorrow. The aware black man understands this. He recognizes that a purely sexual infatuation, like fast foods, can be quick and cheap but won't provide the nutrition needed for a long-term relationship.

Trust between a black man and woman can only be established over a period of time, and its validity can only be attested to during the period. If man does not employ the four Rs, he will never know whether he can trust the woman until it is much too late. Too late for him. Too late for her. Too late for black America.

Can young black males be taught to understand the

four-Rs approach to evaluating a relationship? Can they be trained in the nineties to understand what it means to be a black man? How can the problem of Achilles be solved? The answers to these questions are addressed in the next chapter—about rites of passage programs.

12

Rites of Passage

A father, as head of the family, provided the role model for the young male. The father was seen and understood as the protector, provider, teacher, and disciplinarian. Thirty years ago, the responsible black man was the model and the mentor in the black community. True, although there were negative models, such as pimps with pimpmobiles and gamblers with flashy cars, jewelry, and sexy women, their impressions on black children were minimized by the presence of the strong black man in the family.

If the boy began acting like these negative models, he would be quickly disciplined. The father in Bill Cosby's comic routines was not an uncommon presence in black homes: "Boy, I brought you into this world and if you don't straighten up, I'll take you out of it."

Parenting was a duty, a commitment by the man, a co-responsibility with the woman. It was his job to teach the male child the lessons of life. The male child grew from childhood to manhood under the black man's supervision.

Rick, a businessman in his mid-fifties, describes an incident still vivid in his memory:

"My father pushed me toward manhood when I was eight. I skipped school for three days straight when I was in the third grade. Two of my little buddies and I would play in the cornfield across from school.

"On the third day, my mother found out, but I didn't know it. I came home at 3:15 P.M. just as if I'd been at school. She waited until I was changing my clothes and just when I had my britches off, she came into my room with a switch and wore my little butt out. I mean, she must have whipped me for ten minutes and it was awful. She had never spanked me before; my dad handled the discipline and he could command respect with his belt.

"When Dad came home at dinnertime, I thought I was in for another whipping. I didn't even want to sit at the dinner table, but I did. He didn't say anything to me at dinner and I hurried up and dried the dishes for my mother and ran to my room. I just knew he was going to come in and strap me until I couldn't sit down, but he didn't. I said my prayers real nice and loud for my mother that night. I asked God to bless everybody and help me be a good boy, hoping that my dad wouldn't come in later and whip me. He didn't.

"The next morning, I got up early and dressed for school. Back then, you wore short pants and it was snowing outside and cold. Just as I got to the front hall, my dad walked up to the door and asked me where I was going. I said I was going to school.

"He said, 'Not today, we are going to skip school today.'

"He took my little hand and led me outside to the car, then we rode over to the packing house in Omaha, Nebraska. There, men were carrying half cow carcasses on their backs from the building to the trucks outside. It was cold and snowing as we stood and watched. The men were putting the heavy meat slabs on their shoulders and dragging themselves to the trucks. It felt like we stood out there for hours, but I know it was only for a little while. Then my dad took me up to one of the black men and asked him how far he had gone in school. The man said he left school in the fourth grade, looking at me as he said it.

"About this time I was freezing and ready to go home, but instead Dad put me back in the car and took me over to a coal company in Council Bluffs, Iowa. During those days, car heaters didn't work well in cold weather, they just got lukewarm, so I stayed cold as we drove. At the coal company, we watched a lot of black men shoveling coal into trucks. Again, it seemed like hours passed before my dad took my hand and led me over to a couple of the men, who were all bundled up and wet. He asked both of them to tell me how far they had gone in school. One said he never went to school, as he had to go to work to support his family; the other said he finished sixth grade, but couldn't read.

"We went back to the car and my dad told me that this is the kind of work you do when you don't go to school. He said, 'You see me sitting in a nice, warm office every day, eat in a nice restaurant and take care of you and your mother.' The real lesson came when he told me that I didn't have to go back to school ever again, that I could stop selling papers on Saturdays and get a real job like those men. Before we got home, I was begging my dad to let me go back to school.

"I didn't miss a class again until I was in college, and then only once or twice. My dad knew the men in our family don't like cold weather and we don't like hard, physical work, especially outdoors. He knew which way to take me into manhood and although I still got a lot of spankings after that, it was never for skipping school. He was always there to help me become a man."

For most black boys today, there is no rite of passage from boyhood to manhood. Today's black communities are filled with "boys" in their twenties, thirties, and forties. Who is going to teach today's black boy how to become a black man? Who is going to discipline the black boy? Who is going to protect the black boy as he interacts with his environment? And who is going to show the black boy how a responsible black man should relate to black women?

Not the gangs, not the drug dealers, not the street women. Can black sports and entertainment celebrities be counted on as role models? Get serious! Black boys can't become real men just by being exposed to lifestyles in which the famous wear $200 sneakers, or to extravagant behavior irrelevant to reality and opposed to enduring values.

The solution will come when responsible leaders among black men conduct programs that will reach out to the black boy. Seeds of these programs are beginning to sprout up across the country. Most are still in the formative stage of developing; however, general approaches to conducting these programs have evolved.

Three approaches are *mentoring* programs, *manhood development* programs, and *rites of passage* programs.

Mentoring Programs

In the mentoring programs, the youth are from the inner city, usually the underclass or labor class. The mentors are teachers, ministers, community activists, with a few knowledge-class black men from business and the professions.

The focus is on the guidance of the individual. The ideal arrangement is to have one qualified adult serve as a mentor to one boy. This is similar to the Big Brother program. There usually won't be enough adults for one-to-one mentoring (unless the new one-in-ten leaders come into the program), and the adult who volunteers could have three or four boys to work with. Special activities and outings are planned to allow the mentor to establish rapport with his charges.

One such program has been started by the Board of Education in Chicago. Dr. Clinton Bristow, dean of the Business School at Chicago State College and chairman of the Chicago Board of Education, describes it as Chicago's first attempt to develop a formal mentoring program for inner-city youth through the school system. Bristow began the program in the fall of 1991. All high school principals with their local school councils were requested to plan a mentoring-day program at their school.* "The content and design must be planned and executed to build on

* In Chicago, each school is governed by an elected nonpaying local school board. They make local school policy and select, hire, and fire the school principal, whom they hold responsible for administering the educational program.

the strength and uniqueness of each individual school, its community and local school council," Dr. Bristow says. "I intend to make whatever resources the Board has available to these schools as they conduct their mentoring program. I've suggested, for example, that the alumni of the high schools be contacted and requested to participate in an all-day mentoring program carried out in small black male groups. After this, there would be a pairing of each alumnus with a high school student."

Manhood Development Programs

Manhood development programs focus on the groups rather than on interaction between the mentor and the boy. Generally, there are no criteria for selecting the youth for these programs. Any young black male can be identified and brought to a meeting. A group with a formal organization sets an agenda of meetings and activities that permits members of the organization to teach the recruits about values, discipline, and relations with others. The Five Hundred Blackmen in Chicago, the One Hundred Black Men in California, and BOND (Brother Organization of a New Destiny) in New York are representative of groups that are running successful manhood development programs.

The Five Hundred Blackmen is located in Chicago's South Side. It was formed in the summer of 1990 as a result of a rally to protest an incident involving two black youths and two white police officers. Attendance at the rally exceeded the expected number of two hundred people. The organizers decided to band together to form a permanent group. Attorney Lewis Myers chairs the group, which conducts programs to help young black males become black men.

One of the more recent activities of the Five Hundred Blackmen involved a rally at Bethel AME Church in Chicago. Blackmen brought black youths of all ages to hear what black men were going to do to "reclaim the streets and protect the women and children in the community." More than seven hundred people were in attendance, some men bringing as many as fifteen boys to hear civil rights attorney Thomas N. Todd discuss racial suicide.

SOS (Save Our Sons) is another innovative manhood program. It is entering its third year and is designed and administered by the Reverend Henry Williamson, pastor of Carter Temple C.M.E. Church in Chicago. Every third Sunday at 10:45 A.M., he holds a special worship service only for black men and black boys of all ages. At the end of the service, the two groups form a circle, holding hands, and affirm their commitment to certain principles and values. Although the total membership of the church is approximately one thousand, there are three hundred black men in the congregation, which is a higher male percentage than in many black churches. The SOS program also includes a monthly breakfast or lunch on a Saturday for all the male participants. It is at these gatherings that special themes on values, character, and black men's responsibilities are discussed and explained. Each adult black man is paired off with two or more young males to provide counseling and to carry out individual activities.

Rites of Passage Programs

Mentoring programs, manhood development programs, and rites of passage programs all focus heavily on:

Responsibility.

Values.

Character.

Discipline.

They have the same objectives of getting younger black males mentally and socially closer to strong black men. Each program provides the guidance of responsible black men, but the rites of passage can be distinguished from the other two programs by highly structured meetings, which often include much younger children than those in mentoring or manhood development programs.

Groups like the Urban League and PUSH are beginning to initiate rites of passage programs. PUSH draws heavily from the local communities for support.* In 1991, it conducted sessions to teach young black boys how to be responsible black men. PUSH's rites of passage programs provide responsible black men to meet with young blacks and talk with them about how to deal with the situations they encounter at home, in school, and on the street. The

---

* PUSH also has rites of passage programs for black girls, and certainly should be credited with being very much avant-garde in this area.

manner in which the young people deal with a situation is reviewed and critiqued. These discussions are conducted in groups, as well as on an individual basis.

The second phase of PUSH's program is to encourage churches in the community to adopt a black youth. The church agrees to intercede on the youth's behalf when he is dealing with problems. The church tries to insure that the youth will learn how to "do the right thing" when confronted with a threat to his safety, health, or self-esteem. This program is still too new to evaluate its effectiveness. Nevertheless, it is further evidence that PUSH's focus is turning to proactive confrontation with the "enemy within."

The National Urban League, which supports programs for young unwed mothers, has started a companion program directed at the male partners of these young mothers. James Compton, director of the Chicago Urban League, says that "one of the best ways to help these unwed mothers is for us to help their male partners learn what it is to be a man and teach them how to pass from boyhood to manhood. At least these young mothers can learn what a man is supposed to be and decide if the male they have had sex with can be a man," says Compton. "We have a second program that is funded by the state of Illinois. It's called the Male Responsibility Program. The Urban League conducts this program in the public schools. Presently, it is only in a total of six elementary schools for third and fourth grades one day a week for one hour," he emphasized. "The boys are trained separately in groups, and the focus of the training is on self-esteem, who they are, values, conflict resolution, and role models."

These rites of passage are also too recent to have their

effectiveness measured, but it is obvious that programs like these, no matter how successful they start off, require follow-up programs. The rites of ceremonies, events, and activities can symbolize transition into manhood, but real change won't occur unless there is sustained follow-up and reinforcement.

The Model

Can there be a model for establishing rites of passage programs that include an effective follow-up process? Are there guidelines to insure that black boys complete the passage to responsible manhood? Yes, there are. The model begins with the selection of men to lead the programs. The criteria for the selection are simple:

1. They must have a responsible job.
2. They are active in community affairs.
3. They have an intense desire to assume the survival of black America.
4. They live lives characterized by self-esteem and respect for others.

Training the Leaders

Men selected to lead rites of passage programs should be trained together in three or four formal sessions. The sessions should be led by someone accustomed to conducting this type of activity—teachers, ministers, counselors, or managers from business organizations.

The men selected to direct the training sessions should follow a prescribed method for conducting sessions. The context of their approach will be: "If we don't change now, we face extinction."

In the first session, the trainer must get each member to examine his own life experiences and those around him as these experiences relate to a survival crisis. Valid data and statistics that confirm the critical state of most black lives should be presented. The trainer must confirm that all group members share the same understanding about what the future holds if current conditions continue. He should present the three options for dealing with the present: do nothing, continue to behave in the same manner, or create solutions.

The trainer's objective is to make sure that each member of the group realizes that he will be motivating young men to make drastic behavioral changes. The group must be keenly aware of their own struggles in attaining responsible manhood.

In subsequent sessions (after each member has been sensitized to his own experiences), the leader will assist members in identifying the common ground among themselves. Members must discuss among themselves what actions they could have taken in the past that would have improved their present situation. The trainer will encourage openness by sharing his own experiences in achieving responsible manhood. He must be candid in describing how he confronted "the enemy within."

"What does it mean to be a responsible black man in the nineties?" This should be the topic of one entire training session. Each member's response to this question should be written on a chalkboard or flip stand. After all the responses have been listed, each member should respond to the others' answers. This activity will stimulate the group dynamics in a way that involves each member's commitment to the program.

After the leaders' commitments have been established, the trainer guides the group in determining how they will conduct a rites of passage program. For which age group should the program be intended? How many people can the group accommodate? From what economic classes should the young males come?

Although the general objective will be central to all programs, each program will vary depending on the psychological readiness and the social background of various target groups. The amount of money and number of volunteers available must be considered when determining the scope and extent of a program.

Approaches will be quite different. A group of five- to twelve-year-olds may learn positive values by sharing recreational experiences with black men, while a group of twenty-one- to twenty-six-year-olds may learn positive values through networking, discussion groups, and sponsorships. Although black manhood is found in all classes and can be developed in all classes, a multiclass group will require a different manner of managing group dynamics.*

* To be a responsible black man does not mean to belong to any given class. Malcolm X, who was from the underclass, became a responsible black man while in prison through his experiences. However, it was through his own efforts, self-instruction, and readings that he joined the knowledge class years later, going from a black pimp to black orator, minister, and leader.

If a more formal curriculum is desired, qualified people should be consulted to insure that proper materials are developed.* If the method to attain the specific objectives requires the involvement of counseling or teaching professionals, the leadership group must be precise in determining the extent of their involvement. If part of the program involves life experiences, these activities cannot be too carefully planned. Obviously, the background of participants conducting the program must be scrutinized.

The mentoring process is a necessary part of any ongoing rites of passage program. Each member of the leadership group must serve as a mentor during and after the program. This insures follow-up and reinforcement of the desired attitudes and behavior. A mentor serves as a model, a guide, and an adviser.

The leadership group must consider recognition and rewards to participants in the rites of passage programs. Participants are those who give their time and resources to the program, as well as those for whom the program is intended. The importance of motivators must never be overlooked. They can be the difference between the success or failure of the program.

When the rites of passage program has been completed, there must be both a follow-up phase and a give-back

* The degree or amount of Afrocentric content included in the program will depend upon the comfort zone of the self-help group. To reflect African culture is not the primary or secondary objective of the rites of passage. Those who feel that such content helps them teach self-esteem and manhood should use it if it helps the self-help group achieve its objectives of their rites of passage programs.

phase. These two phases reinforce the lessons and provide feedback about the program's effectiveness.

The give-back phase should focus on encouraging those who completed the program to serve as big brothers to young males who weren't in such a program. Those who are on the road to responsible manhood should be expected to contribute to their community, their families, and to future rites of passage programs.

Rites of passage programs, mentoring, and manhood development programs won't save all the black men who haven't achieved responsible adulthood, but they will increase the number of black men who do achieve it. These programs will reduce the number of casualties on the black man's death row. These programs will produce the strong black leaders to confront the problems that prevent the rise of an economically sound black America.

CHAPTER

13

In the Meantime

This book's first three sentences in chapter 1 say:

"The plight of the vanishing black American male, which is contributing to the diminishing number of healthy black American families, is a major domestic problem in America. It is not a problem that can be solved by the federal government, or even by a majority of the population working toward a solution.

"The main obstacle is that the problem has its own problem, that of a segment of our people who fail to recognize that there's a problem in the first place."

A threat to national security is an American problem. A threat to due process is an American problem. *But the reluctance of a group of people to help themselves is their problem.*

One of the intents of this book is to convince the reader of this premise. The survival of black America depends on:

(1) all black Americans accepting responsibility for their own behavior and (2) being courageous enough not to condone behavior that destroys their communities.

The same energy, courage, and dedication that blacks brought to the civil rights movement must be brought to bear on raising the standards of behavior in the black community.

A great debt is owed to black Americans of thirty years ago, who risked everything to raise America's awareness of racial injustice. Will black Americans, thirty years from now, be proud of today's blacks, whom I suggest should risk everything to preserve black families, black communities, and black American heritage?

Are black Americans ready to face the "enemy within" with the same commitment that yesterday's blacks had when they confronted Eugene "Bull" Connor?* Is not a Sapphire or an Achilles more dangerous to black lives than dogs and fire hoses?

Gangs, trafficking in drugs, have automatic weapons. But would such gangs exist if there was no market for drugs? Moreover, will the responsible, "aware" black man join such a gang that was financed by selling drugs that kill?

What change in our elected leaders would we accomplish if we stopped talking about entitlements and focused on who really gains from poverty programs run by the federal government?

The late actor Peter Finch won an Oscar for his perfor-

---

* Eugene "Bull" Connor was the chief of police in Birmingham, Alabama. His police officers used dogs and fire hoses to attack blacks participating in a 1963 civil rights protest in Birmingham.

mance as the stressed-out TV anchorman in the movie *Network*. The highlight of this award-winning performance occurs when he exhorts his viewers to shout, "I'm mad as hell and I'm not going to take it anymore!" What better words can concerned black Americans shout to the brothers and sisters who won't take responsibility for their actions.

Confront the enemies within with these words, and back them up with action. Conduct your lives so that you earn the trust and respect of your community. Live in the glass house. Insist that parents parent, teachers teach, and preachers preach (while practicing what they preach).

Change

If black Americans confront the enemies within, there will be a new day "by 'n' by." Confronting the enemies within demands a change in attitudes about ourselves and about some institutions. A radical change in attitude toward two systems is absolutely necessary. The systems are welfare and education. Plus a new approach to revitalizing marriages with a bold new approach based on an old European peasant philosophy.

Welfare

The underclass must be weaned from the present system of welfare, a system that evolved from compassion to become a major factor in the disintegration of the black family. It has become a lifestyle rather than a temporary support system or the means of assisting families as they work to better their condition.

There are more whites than blacks on welfare, but in percentages, the ratio of whites doesn't come close to the number of blacks on welfare. In most of these black families, welfare has produced second-, third-, and fourth-generation welfare recipients.

On January 30, 1992, the *MacNeil/Lehrer NewsHour* interviewed a black woman and one of her daughters, an eight-year-old. When the mother was asked how long she had been on welfare, she responded, "On and off for eighteen years." When she was asked why she hadn't gotten a job during this time, she said she "tried a couple of times, but the government took too much out of my paycheck. I get more by being on welfare." When the daughter was asked what welfare was, she said, "That's when people give you money." When asked why people gave them money, the little girl's reply was " 'Cause they have to." When asked if she was ashamed or felt bad about being on welfare, the girl said "No."

There are those who would argue statistics rather than analyze attitudes. They say that the average welfare mother has only two children. What they don't quote is the large increase in the number of welfare mothers with two children or the increase in second-, third-, and fourth-generation welfare mothers.

When an employed person has a child, he or she does not automatically get a raise. If they have four children in eight years, they still don't get a raise every time they announce the birth of another baby, more child care costs, food bills, and clothing costs. They get paid for what they do on the job, not for producing more babies at home. If they lose their jobs, they receive unemployment income, temporary funds to tide them over to their next job. If they don't get a job in a prescribed amount of time, they become homeless. The welfare system operates in reverse.

A black woman on welfare with one child for eight years earns less than another black woman on welfare with four children over the same eight years. The message is clear. As a single parent, if you want more money, have more babies. Prior to 1960, most black women were part of a nuclear family. In the underclass, the black family is now a myth. Unfortunately, the myth was created by the present welfare system. It's not Aid to *Families* with Dependent Children but a lifetime annuity to women *using* dependent children.

Well-meaning people argue that decreasing welfare payments puts the dependent children at risk of malnutrition or even starvation. They don't understand that the present system has contributed to an environment that exposes a child to greater risks. These babies become destined for failure before they get to school. Children are raped, killed, or sent to prison, not because there is no financial safety net, but because the present system won't accommodate the development of emotional safety nets.

It is the children, not in small numbers, who are used and abused. Children held in hostage. Sympathizers argue that without AFDC, Aid to Families with Dependent Children, many children would starve, go without clothing, and die from malnutrition. That is happening all over this country anyway in varying degrees with the present welfare system.

Front page: nineteen kids were found in a Chicago

hovel last night. Six women, ages twenty to twenty-five, and two men occupied the apartment at 219 Keystone Avenue. All children were under the age of nine except for one fourteen-year-old. Filthy clothes and rotting food littered the West Side apartment, while nineteen cold, hungry children huddled on bare mattresses, wearing soiled diapers and dirty underwear, fighting over a gnarled bone with the family dog. A postscript: The mothers collectively were receiving $4,000 monthly in welfare aid.

This is children held hostage. This country never gives into hostage demands, since it knows that never solves the problem. Why then give in to it in welfare and not in warfare? These mothers, who have nineteen children among them, expect and sometimes demand the ransom—$4,000—so the children won't die. The children would be better off as hostages in a foreign country than they are at 219 Keystone Avenue! They are casualties of a war on the ways of a subculture and people with a certain mind-set. If there have to be casualties, why not casualties directed at ending those ways and mind-set? The present AFDC system encourages it. What about those females and males who sacrifice having children so that they don't have to live on welfare all their lives? Not all women from this culture have babies, although that doesn't get the same media attention. What is the present policy of the welfare system telling these women? "If you want to have some money in your pocket today, have some babies" is the message. It feeds the Sapphire syndrome.

More babies. More money. Children held hostage. What is needed is a welfare system that removes the ransom and gets rid of the hostage taker. The present welfare system shows a Keystone Kops mentality. Well intended, but silly and dumb.

The present system perpetuates the fallacy that welfare recipients will always be poor. Immigrants coming into this country from Europe, Asia, and Eastern nations are *broke*, not poor. They come here looking for freedom and opportunity. Once they arrive in America, they do what is necessary to support their families. They do not have an attitude of "poor." They are not hampered by the welfare mentality of dependence. The leaders in new immigrant communities will provide temporary assistance, but they also encourage new arrivals to work. The new arrivals are given the opportunity to learn how to improve their economic status. They understand that "broke" is merely a temporary condition.

Understanding the difference between an attitude of "poor" or an attitude of "broke" determines what a person will do to help himself or herself. Those people who succeeded with the help of the War on Poverty had the "I'm broke, not poor" attitude. They believed in and looked for the opportunity to work toward a better economic status.

Because it is overloaded, the present system of welfare will of necessity be reduced. During the sixties, America, the land of plenty, experienced an affluent middle class, no budget deficits, and faced a future of unlimited prosperity. The haves felt guilty and, led by the liberal movement, most Americans did not mind paying higher taxes for what they thought was the noble cause of assisting the less fortunate.

Now the concern of the typical American is how to maintain a quality of life for himself and his family.

Welfare money comes from the people who work and build businesses. When working citizens have to choose between maintaining the quality of life for their families or maintaining the present welfare system, their choice is obvious, particularly because of the abuse of the welfare system. Already, thirteen states in the United States have reduced their general assistance budgets.* The state of Michigan in 1991 totally ended its general assistance welfare program for ninety thousand residents and saved $247 million.† Monies to welfare mothers are being reduced in many states. New Jersey's then governor Jim Florio signed into law a series of bills making New Jersey the first state to deny additional welfare benefits to recipients who have children while receiving public aid. Similar measures are being considered in California.

Civil rights and black community groups should lead the movement to change the welfare system. They should support legislation similar to New Jersey's and Michigan's, but they should also make sure that there are countermeasures taken. For example, they could help implement an adjustable welfare program. In such a program, the mother with one child should be given an adjustable income based on cost of living and inflation. This would last for a limited period of time, for example, while she took training or gained work experience in the form of public service work.

* General assistance is the money budgeted by each state to pay single adults who indicate they cannot work or take employment for some physical or mental problem.
† *Chicago Tribune*, October 2, 1991, sec. 1, p. 2.

If the mother has a second child during the time that she is receiving the money, the welfare system would not increase her income unless she marries the father of the child. She made the decision to have another child and she and her man must assume the responsibility. If they marry and he is unemployed, both he and she would receive assistance for a defined period of time during which he must get a meaningful job. If they separate or divorce during this period, the joint assistance ends and she will be placed back on the one-child program with the same termination date she had when she first entered the program. The father will be required to support the second child or face prosecution. If the woman has several more illegitimate children, she is only qualified to get payments under the one-child, limited-term program.

The present cost of welfare would be less if the monies were used to place children in other homes, homes administered and run by community, church, and civil rights groups. If a mother continues to demonstrate that she does not care about the welfare of her children, her conduct should be treated as a child abuse case.

When black groups develop innovative programs to care for children of negligent mothers, they are establishing family support systems. These family support systems can provide the guidance, love, and discipline now lacking in most welfare households.

Churches and civil rights groups can solicit the aid of responsible black men and women to work in these family care programs as role model parents. Children can be housed, fed, and loved in an environment that teaches them the role and benefits of two-parent families. Money saved from not rewarding illegitimacy can finance jobs in these programs and even finance employment for those mothers who sincerely want to help themselves. Administrative and operational expenses should be paid to those groups sponsoring such programs.

This chapter is not intended as a political blueprint for building or overhauling the welfare system. It is intended to provoke innovation. The pragmatic approaches described here are only some examples of what can be done to remove the addiction of welfare dependency and enhance the future of black children.

Education

The American public school system historically evolved from communities where two-parent homes and steady employment were the norm. These systems were not designed to transmit knowledge to children who have learned "all the wrong lessons" before their first day in the schoolroom.

In most urban areas, schools are struggling with a situation that puts them into the unfortunate position of trying to effect change in children's behavior. But they fail to do so for many reasons. One is the size and the composition of the classes. In inner-city schools, there are too many students per classroom. The problem of the crowded classroom is compounded by the presence of both boys and girls, young black children who have already learned how to entice, provoke, and aggravate each other.

Some school systems attempted to solve the problems resulting from having boys and girls in the same classroom by establishing all-male schools. The foci of such schools are on personal discipline, civic responsibility, high academic standards, and African-American history. The Milwaukee and Detroit public school systems attempted to establish such schools in 1991 but both encountered resistance from opponents of an all-male concept.

The American Civil Liberties Union (ACLU) and the National Organization of Women (NOW) Legal Defense and Education Fund brought suit against the Detroit school board stating that this denied girls access to quality programs. The court found in favor of the ACLU and NOW, stating that such an arrangement would violate the Constitution's equal protection guarantee and those of Title IX of the 1972 Education Act.

Supporters of all-black-male schools counter that all kinds of single-sex special schools exist. There are those for pregnant girls, borderline incorrigible boys, and black boys who have special needs.

There are some black educators who are attempting to develop an option to the black male academies by setting up all-black-male classrooms. Dr. Spencer Holland supervises two "boys only" classes at Robert W. Coleman Elementary School in Baltimore. Dr. Holland's first all-boy classroom at Matthew Henson Elementary School in Baltimore is now four years old.

Another such school is West Side Tilton in Chicago. The principal, Jesse Moore, has one fifth-grade class made up of all boys. "We thought fifth grade was a good place to start," he explains. "Most of the older boys are already lost." John Grey, the teacher of this twenty-eight-boy class, says, "It's called corporate learning. We try to instill in them that they can work together." This program has support both from the local school council as well as community parents. There is a waiting list for those parents who want their boys enrolled in the program.

Nationally, less than 2 percent of the elementary school teachers are black men. Even if the school districts attempted to establish all-male classrooms or black male academies, they could not, at present, be staffed by black male teachers. In Norfolk, Virginia, at Bowling Park Elementary School, Dr. Herman Clark set up separate classrooms for boys in kindergarten and the fifth grade. The teacher, Ann Chruscilel, is white. Dr. Clark, a black principal, has no black male teachers, a problem that is common to all public schools. The adaptability of public schools is limited by resources and bureaucracies.

Private education programs are emerging that meet the need of the black male child. These programs are being financed, administered, and controlled by blacks. If blacks want to structure schools around black male classes, these emerging programs provide an opportunity to do so. If blacks will pay the cost, they can be the boss. They won't have to ask permission to educate their children differently from the public educational systems. Blacks won't have to let outside organizations, like the ACLU, NOW, or government agencies, block their efforts to help their young black males learn what is necessary to become black men. The outside organizations must forget their narrow agendas and consider the fact that this is a temporary measure to get black back on track.

The University of Islam is one of the more successful private programs. It is located on the South Side of Chicago and is in its fourth year of operation. They boys attend all-male classes in the morning and leave the building before the girls come to school for classes in the afternoon. Although each group attends school for only a half-day, both groups receive as much academic training as public school students in Chicago. Each half-day session is devoted solely to academics. There are no gym, recess, or snack breaks.

From preschoolers to high schoolers, these boys wear blue pants, white shirts, bow ties, dark socks and shoes. Discipline, values, character, and respect are taught to all of these children in addition to the academic curriculum. "Yes, sir" and "No, sir" is the respectful way that the students are taught to verbally respond to the faculty. The faculty addresses the students with similar respect.

Disrespect is not tolerated. Absence is excused only after verifying a legitimate reason with a parent or guardian. Ms. Shelbey Muhammad, the principal of the school, says, "The boys and girls are educated separately and are never in each other's presence during school." The primary reason for this is: "There is such a strong attraction between young black males and young black females that it often interferes with the learning process."

Parents are required to pay $1,640 per year for one child and $640 for each additional child. Parents do not have to be of the Muslim faith, but they are required to participate in the parents' association and attend all association meetings. The children travel to and from school in twos if their parents do not provide transportation. Gang activity is forbidden, and this rule is strictly enforced.

The effectiveness of the University of Islam's approach to educating black children is apparent when one observes the children in and out of the classroom. In the classroom, they are attentive, respectful, alert, and active. Outside the classroom, they act in a disciplined manner and reflect a considerable degree of self-control.

Civil rights organizations and church and community groups can copy this existing model. It is not the Muslim religion that made this program a success. It is because of the empowerment that a group of concerned blacks have obtained by taking the initiative. They built a program that the public education system couldn't provide.

Other black educators can demonstrate the same commitment and work toward more independent programs where black boys can be educated separately. Frank Hayden in Detroit and Spencer Holland in Baltimore have demonstrated to all blacks that where there is a will, there is a way.

The time of the citizens of a black community is better spent establishing innovative programs than demonstrating in the streets about what the public school system can't do.

Marriage: A New Philosophy

When immigrants come to our shores in search of a new life, the adults, often with little education and skills, understand that for the family to succeed so that future generations may prosper, it is necessary for one generation to be sacrificed. This is true whether the new immigrants are Hungarian, Bosnian, Mexican, or Nicaraguan.

Some of these immigrants may even be from the knowledge class. For example, there are Russian immigrants to the United States who are attorneys, doctors, physicists, even journalists. Because of language, often poorer training (medicine), different legal systems, these people still come here with their families, knowing the difficulties they will face. Why? Because they are seeking opportunities for their children.

Of course, there are universal professions in which language is no barrier, such as the fields of music, dance, art, and athletics. In these, they have a chance to prosper almost immediately.

To put the matter more bluntly, do blacks have the courage and capacity to sacrifice one generation to allow the black race to survive? What does it entail? It all started with the 1 million black men who served in World War II and subsequent wars. This allowed black women to leave poor-paying domestic jobs to enter (1) the workplace and (2) the halls of higher education.

Are the better-educated black women willing to go to war to help the black man? Are they now willing to marry less-educated black men in order to create homes and black families for the survival of the race? The sacrifice would be one generation.

By giving black males a hand up to a better life, families would be able to reverse the trend of the past four decades, and the blacks will be back on track. Are black males worth the sacrifice? Many are. Some probably aren't. But it has to start somewhere. It can be made to work. No woman should consider that she is marrying "down" . . . when she is building "up" and healing wounds that are destroying black America. In reality, it's payback time.

Rebuilding black America has to start somewhere—not by gender hatred, not by blaming whitey, but with a new pioneer spirit, a crusade leading into the future. Reclaim family values and family life. Get more ministers to stop talking and start doing. Nurture our one-in-ten leaders forecast by W. E. B. Du Bois. Create a new black America.

Blacks can change their lives. They can stop welfare dependency, and they can establish their own schools. Encourage black people to confront their problems, not blame others. Change ingrained attitudes, and question the viability of present-day attitudes. Create a corps of leaders.

The next chapter discusses what attributes characterize this new breed.

Dreams and Visions

The previous chapters plead for black America to take action characterized by the same courage and commitment shown in the civil rights movement of the sixties.

Overcoming today's enemies from within requires sorts of leadership roles different from those that led the good fight against yesterday's outside enemies.

Dr. Martin Luther King, Jr., and Malcolm X had dreams, but neither lived long enough to turn their dreams into visions. "I have a dream" was a beginning, but fell far short of "I have a vision." Today's black leaders must become visualizers and actualizers. They must visualize black men taking control of their own lives and families. They must devise plans to assure their attainment of this control.

In black communities across this great nation, most blacks have no plan about what black men must do to deliver themselves from today's dilemma. Instead of a plan, there are demands, pleas, and calls for more studies. What results are more words and no action. A plan is a blueprint for action. First comes the vision, next comes the plan, then comes the action.

The civil rights movement was a reaction to the racist practices of the time. Although the focus was on civil rights, many blacks dreamed of social equality. Part of the dream was that blacks would be able to sit anywhere on a bus as they traveled to work. They realized that dream.

The civil rights movement will remain a proud chapter in our nation's history. The country is stronger, more viable, and more worthy of allegiance because of it. The fact remains that too few black Americans have taken advantage of the other opportunities the movement achieved.

Visions, unlike dreams, are dynamic and are often the products of an active mind. Visions may be insights into the future or enable people to challenge accepted beliefs and replace them with new ones. A vision is an insight of the intellect. The person with a vision is one who will act, not react.

In 1991, Operation PUSH attempted a boycott by black Americans of buying Nike shoes. The purpose of the boycott was to force the Nike company to appoint a black to its board of directors, use a black-owned bank for some of its transactions, and hire a black-owned advertising agency.

Operation PUSH justified the attempted boycott by citing the fact that many black youths were buying the high-priced Nike shoes. PUSH "reasoned" that since blacks accounted for a significant part of Nike's sales, then blacks should share in the business.

To no one's surprise (except PUSH's), the attempted boycott of Nike products failed. Reactive efforts like this attempted boycott are designed (inadvertently) to fail. Nike was a successful business conducting its affairs in a legal and ethical manner. They had developed a line of high-quality products that were in great demand. There was no evidence of Nike practicing racial discrimination toward their employees, their suppliers, or their customers. Their shoes were available for resale at retail outlets without regard to skin color of the retailer or where he conducted his business.

People with vision would have *acted* differently after assessing Nike's success. They would not have made demands with the statement "You owe us." Visionary leaders would have focused their attention on the dynamics of the sneaker business. There would be a *plan* to capitalize on the growing demand for sneakers and seek business opportunities in athletic footwear (and accessories, competing brands, retail outlets, distribution networks, etc.). A well-reasoned business plan led by visionary people would attract capital from black and white investors.

As stated earlier, the problems facing black Americans as discussed in this book are not government problems, and do not require government solutions. They're black America's problems and black America's challenge.

Index